Hot AND Co
SOUPS

How about a delightful iced soup to cool the palate on a very hot and stressful day? Or just sit around the pool, relax with a good book, and you will find that an iced soup is just the ticket to get the taste buds going. Try our Gazpacho with just a hint of chilli or a creamy Vichyssoise to soothe the nerves.

Hot AND Cold SOUPS

Thick hearty soups for the cold months
and cold refreshing soups for the hot months.

Junita Doidge

NEW HOLLAND

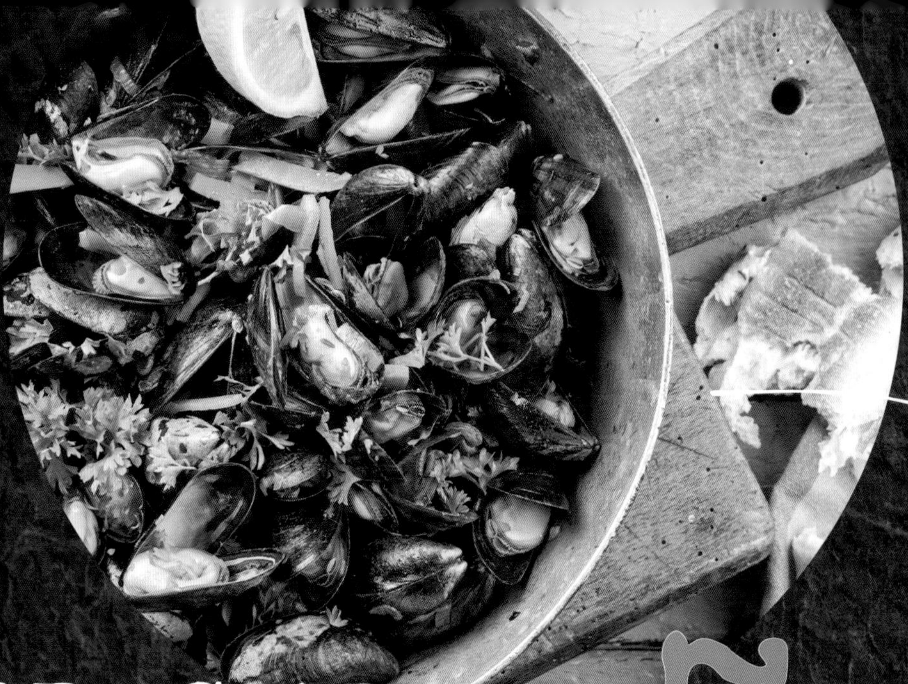

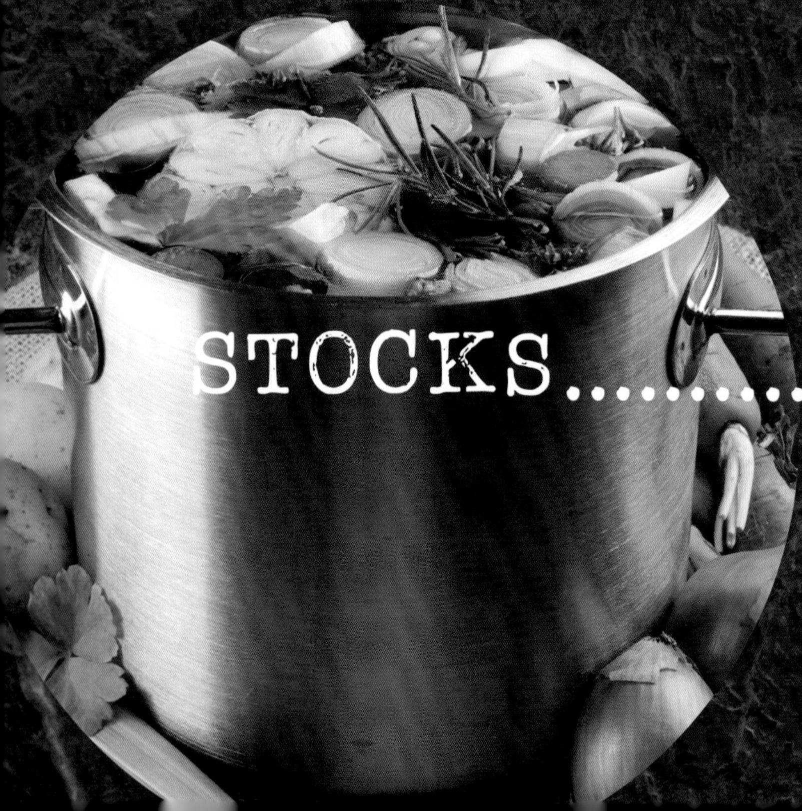

CONTENTS

INTRODUCTION

Soup is one of the most basic foods. Its history stretches far into the past when soup was simply water simmered with whatever basic ingredients were available for flavour. Soup then was never about quality ingredients and complex flavours. Rather, it was simply about survival. Yet soup was still a meal shared between family members and acquaintances. Thick hearty soups are served in the cold months to nourish and satisfy hungry children and to give energy to people at the end of a hectic day. Cold refreshing soups are served in hot weather and humid climates to invigorate and enliven after an exhausting day.

Throughout the Western world soups are served as a teaser to the coming meal, while in China soup is served after a meal as an invigorating finale. In many European countries soup is served between courses to refresh the palate. In fact, soup is served more often and in many more flavour combinations throughout the world than any other meal.

Soups have changed in many ways over the years, with modern cooking methods and ingredients taking over from traditional methods and ingredients. What would Great Grandpa have said if Great Grandma had served him up a soup of onions cooked in white wine and brandy? The very idea! Soups made from rockmelon and peaches. Soups with Japanese liqueur in them. Soups served chilled! Ah yes times have changed.

It could be argued that the level of a nation's culinary sophistication can be seen in the soups it serves. There's nothing wrong with good old traditionals like beef shin or calf's foot, however we tend now to use more modern ingredients.

The modern cook prefers to stay away from the predictable and concentrate on a selection of recipes that use imaginative ingredients in imaginative ways. In the recipe selection offered in these chapters we include, with the traditional, some delightful variations.

When planning your dinner party, choose your soup carefully. A dinner of several courses should be preceded by a light clear soup, preferably a consommé. Thick soups, on the other hand, should be regarded as part of the main meal. And, of course, fruit soups may be served before or after the meal.

Soups are time-honoured comfort foods, with well-rounded flavours and soothing, sustained warmth. Prepared more often in a single pot, they can incorporate all kinds of ingredients in combinations that are as nutritious as they are delicious.

Be lost in a sense of well-being as the contents of your cooking pot boil and bubble and the tendrils of steam and aroma curl up, permeating the surroundings and inducing a real warmth and homely feeling. What dreary winter afternoon is not brightened by the companionable murmur of a simmering soup on the stove?

A soup can be thick or thin, it can range from a clear, light broth to a hearty chowder almost thick enough to eat with a knife and fork. It has been noted that several centuries ago soup was served over five courses as a total meal.

At the turn of the century it was normal to have soup always be served as part of the evening meal. These days however, we are not as regimented and soup can be served at any time of the night or day and in almost any position on the menu – from snack to main course, from entrée to dessert. Or indeed, soups can, and sometimes do, constitute an entire meal.

Our selected recipes offer soups of all types for all occasions and are built upon one of the basic stock recipes that appear in this introduction. Most are simple to prepare and in most situations require a minimum investment in time. Of course, we offer slow-cooked soups as well as some real fast heat and serve varieties - truly a selection of recipes to suit all appetites and tastes.

TECHNIQUES

While soup is very easy to make and delightfully satisfying to eat, there is no doubt that a few tricks of the trade and some handy hints will give you superior results, even if you have never made a pot of soup before.

COOKWARE

While quality cookware is always a joy to use, remember that soups are centuries old and most of our ancestors didn't have the pleasure of shiny new cookware and elegant stovetops. Just use whatever large saucepans or stockpots you have. If you find you need a new saucepan, purchase a high-quality pot with a strong enamel or non-stick surface, or a stainless steel pot that has an insulated base. Cast iron works well too.

INGREDIENTS

We all want to use the best, freshest ingredients when we prepare foods for our family or friends, and there is no doubt that quality ingredients contribute towards a more delicious and healthy end result. Meat, fish, poultry, spices and herbs should always be in peak condition for the best soups. Vegetables, however, can be a little wilted or past their prime. When you are about to make a soup or stock, clean out your vegetable crisper and see what has been left behind. Of course, common-sense should prevail, so don't use any vegetables that smell unpleasant or are obviously mouldy.

Note: Most soups freeze well. When freezing any liquid, leave a 5mm space between the soup and the lid of the container, as liquid expands during freezing.

HOME-MADE STOCKS – FOUNDATIONS OF FLAVOUR

The basis of a quality soup is a quality stock – it's as simple as that! In years past, a good soup always began with hours of simmering simple vegetables and, perhaps, some meat bones to create a rich broth. These days, however, if you prefer to bypass this step, there are several prepared stocks available from your local supermarket. They can be found in liquid form, as a paste or as a powder. Generally speaking, it is much easier to purchase liquid stocks as they have a true flavour and are litreally ready to use. Pastes are a good option too because they are concentrated, which allows you to add as much water as necessary to dilute the flavour according to your tastes.

In our opinion, most stock powders should be avoided if the liquid or paste stocks are available. These powders are often heavily salted and therefore offer a salty rather than 'true to taste' flavour. The ratio of powder to water can be difficult to master and some brands contain artificial flavours and colours. By far the most rewarding and delicious stock is the one you make yourself. Contrary to popular belief, stocks are not difficult to make and, although they do need to simmer for quite some time, their preparation time is minimal.

The following recipes will guide you through the basics of making a good stock – regardless of which type of stock you wish to make, you can follow one of these basic methods. If you have any vegetables in your refrigerator that are looking a little wilted and sad, throw these into the stockpot too as they will add extra flavour and colour. Oh, and one other thing – remember that stocks freeze extremely well for extended periods of time, so don't be afraid to make a pot of stock when you have large amounts of vegetables, roasted meat bones or turkey frames (from the Christmas bird) on hand. Make the stock and pop it in the freezer for your future risotto or soup.

Making good stock is a very simple procedure. The ingredients are simmered in a pot – when strained and degreased the cooking liquid becomes a savoury essence to serve on its own, store for later use, or use in preparing another dish. Recipes for the five basic stocks follow on the next pages. Stock comes from humble beginnings – inexpensive cuts of meat and bones, fish bones and heads, or chicken wings and backs. Attention to detail will reward you with a rich and tasty stock. All large fat deposits should be removed beforehand, but large bones will give you treasured gelatine, if cracked first, and provide body to your stock. During cooking, remove scum that occasionally collects on top of the liquid. Scum consist of protein particles released by meat and bones, these float to the surface, where they gather in a foam. As nutritious as it is, the foam must be removed lest it cloud the stock. Skim off the foam as it forms at the start of cooking, skim thereafter only as the recipe directs.

After its initial rapid cooking, stock must not be allowed to return to rapid boil as the turbulence will muddy the liquid. As a final cleansing, the stock should be strained through a fine sieve or a colander lined with muslin.

STOCKS

The basis of a quality soup is a quality stock – it's as simple as that! In years past, a good soup always began with hours of simmering simple vegetables and, perhaps some meat bones, to create a rich broth.

Rich Vegetable Stock

SUGGESTED INGREDIENTS

2 tablespoons olive oil

1 turnip or swede

5 cloves garlic

3 stalks celery

3 large carrots

10 mushrooms

3 large onions

4 tomatoes

2 leeks, well washed

2 parsnips

10 sprigs parsley

1 teaspoon peppercorns

8 Brussels sprouts

4 bay leaves

METHOD

1. Wash all the vegetables and slice or chop roughly.

2. Heat the olive oil in a large stockpot and sauté all the vegetables for 20 minutes until they begin to develop a golden colour on the surface.

3. Add the parsley, peppercorns, bay leaves and water to cover (about 4 litres /135.3 fl oz) and bring to the boil. Simmer for 3 hours, skimming the surface to remove any scum that accumulates.

4. Add salt to taste, then simmer for a further few minutes if you would like a more intense flavour. Allow to cool then strain, pressing on the solids. Use within three days or freeze for up to 12 months.

In addition to the vegetables below, you can add any other vegetables in your refrigerator that are past their prime - greens, root vegetables, corn and capsicum all work well.

Hot & Cold Soups

Chicken Stock

MAKES 10 CUPS

SUGGESTED INGREDIENTS

2 carrots

1 turnip or swede

4 stalks celery

3 onions

1 leek, chopped

8 sprigs parsley, chopped

2 kg (4 lb 8 oz) chicken frames or wings

1 teaspoon peppercorns

4 bay leaves

METHOD

1. Wash all the vegetables and slice or chop roughly.
2. Place all ingredients in a large stockpot. Add water to generously cover the ingredients (about 4 litres / 135.3 fl oz). Bring to the boil then simmer for 2–3 hours, skimming the scum off the surface as it rises to the top.
3. Add salt to taste, then strain the stock through a sieve lined with absorbent paper or cheesecloth.
4. Place in a large saucepan and chill until the fat solidifies on the surface. Remove the fat and use or freeze the stock.

Fish Stock

MAKES 4 CUPS

SUGGESTED INGREDIENTS

500 g (1 lb 2 oz) fish bones, heads and trimmings, washed

2 carrots, chopped

4 stalks celery, chopped

3 onions, roughly chopped

8 sprigs parsley, chopped

6 white peppercorns

good pinch of ground nutmeg

1 teaspoon salt

METHOD

1. Place the fish pieces and 4 cups (35 fl oz) water into a saucepan and bring to the boil.

2. Skim off any discoloured froth from the top. Add remaining ingredients and simmer gently, uncovered, for a further 30 minutes. If cooked too long the stock becomes bitter.

3. Strain and discard the bones and vegetables. Use the stock within two days or freeze it in a sealed container.

Hot & Cold Soups

Prawn (Shrimp) Stock

MAKES
4
CUPS

SUGGESTED INGREDIENTS

1 kg (2 lb 4 oz) prawn (shrimp) shells and heads

2 carrots

4 stalks celery

3 onions

1 leek

8 sprigs parsley, chopped

1 teaspoon peppercorns

METHOD

1. Thoroughly wash shells and heads.

2. Wash all the vegetables and slice or chop roughly, then place in a large stockpot with the shells, parsley and peppercorns. Cover with cold water (about 4 litres /135.3 fl oz), bring to the boil and simmer for 1–2 hours, skimming the scum off the surface as it rises to the top.

3. Add salt to taste, then strain through a sieve lined with absorbent paper or cheesecloth.

4. Place in a large saucepan and chill until the fat solidifies on the surface. Remove the fat and use or freeze the stock.

Veal Stock

MAKES 10 CUPS

SUGGESTED INGREDIENTS

1 kg (2lb 4 oz) veal breast or veal shin meat, cut into 75mm (3 in) pieces

2 kg (4 lb 8 oz) veal bones (preferably knuckles), cracked

2 carrots

4 stalks celery

3 onions

4 sprigs fresh thyme, leaves removed and stalks discarded

2 sprigs of fresh rosemary

3 unpeeled cloves garlic, crushed

8 black peppercorns

1 bay leaf

METHOD

1. Fill a large stock pot halfway with water. Bring the water to the boil, add the veal meat and bones, and blanch them for 2 minutes to clean them.

2. Drain the meat and bones in a colander, discard the liquid. Rinse the meat and bones under cold running water and return them to the pot.

3. Wash all the vegetables and slice or chop roughly. Then place in a large stockpot with the veal bones and meat and all remaining ingredients.

4. Cover with cold water (about 4 litres / 135.3 fl oz), bring to the boil and simmer for 2–3 hours, skimming the scum off the surface as it rises to the top.

5. Add salt to taste, then strain through a sieve lined with absorbent paper or cheesecloth.

6. Place in a large saucepan and chill until the fat solidifies on the surface. Remove the fat and use or freeze the stock.

Hot & Cold Soups

Brown stock

MAKES
10
CUPS

INGREDIENTS

1 kg (2 lb 4 oz) veal breast or beef or veal shin meat, cut into 75 mm (3 in) pieces

2 kg (4 lb 6 oz) veal or beef bones, cracked

2 carrots, chopped

4 stalks celery, chopped

3 onions, chopped

3 unpeeled cloves garlic, crushed

8 black peppercorns

3 cloves

4 sprigs fresh thyme, leaves removed and stalks discarded

1 bay leaf

METHOD

1. Preheat oven to 220°C (420°F), place meat, bones, carrots, celery and onions in a large roasting pan and roast for about 1 hour, until well browned.

2. Transfer the contents of the roasting pan to a large saucepan. Pour 2 cups (17 fl oz) of water into the roasting pan and, with a spatula, scrape up all the brown bits from the bottom and sides of the pan. Pour this liquid into the large saucepan.

3. Add the garlic, peppercorns and cloves. Pour in enough water to cover the contents of the saucepan by about 75 mm (3 in). Bring to the boil, then reduce heat to a simmer and skim off any impurities from the surface. Add the thyme and bay leaf, then simmer the stock for about 4 hours, skimming occasionally.

4. When cooked, strain the stock, allow to cool and refrigerate. You can later degrease the stock by lifting the congealed fat from the surface.

5. If you are making a consommé, which must be served fat-free, lightly draw an ice cube over the surface of the stock, the fat will cling to the cube. Alternatively, blot up any fat with absorbent paper.

HOT SOUPS

There is nothing like the delicious aroma of home-made soup wafting through your home. The only thing that comes close is the satisfaction you feel when you have made a sensational soup all by yourself! The only difficult thing about these recipes is deciding which one to cook first.

Provençal-style soup with onion pesto

SERVES 4-6

INGREDIENTS

2 tablespoons extra virgin olive oil

1 onion, chopped

1 medium potato, peeled and chopped

1 carrot, chopped

1 yellow capsicum (bell pepper), deseeded and chopped

500 ml (17 fl oz) vegetable stock

2 stalks celery, chopped

2 zucchini (courgette), chopped

400 g (14 oz) canned chopped tomatoes

1 tablespoon tomato purée

sea salt and freshly ground black pepper

METHOD

1. For the soup, heat the oil in a large heavy-based saucepan, then add the onion, potato, carrot and yellow capsicum. Cook uncovered for 5 minutes over a medium heat, stirring occasionally, until the vegetables just start to brown.

2. Add the stock, celery and courgette and bring to the boil. Cover and simmer for 10 minutes or until the vegetables are tender. Stir in the tomatoes, tomato purée and season generously. Simmer uncovered for 10 minutes.

3. Meanwhile, make the pesto. Place the spring onion, Parmesan and oil in a food processor and process together to a fairly smooth paste. Ladle the soup into bowls and top with a spoonful of the pesto.

ONION PESTO

6 spring onions (scallions), roughly chopped

50 g (1¾ oz) Parmesan, grated

4 tablespoons extra virgin olive oil

Borscht

SERVES
8

INGREDIENTS

4 medium beetroots

4 cups (35 fl oz) chicken stock

1 onion, peeled and studded with 4 cloves

1 bouquet garni

1 tablespoon sugar

1 tablespoon lemon juice

salt

¼ cup (2 fl oz) sour cream

METHOD

1. Peel and slice 3 of the beetroots. Cook in the stock with onion and bouquet garni until quite tender. Cook the remaining beetroot, without peeling, in boiling water until tender. Allow to cool, peel and grate or cut into julienne strips.

2. Remove herbs and onion and purée cooked beetroot. Add sugar, lemon juice, salt and the grated beetroot to the purée. Chill thoroughly. Garnish with a spoonful of sour cream and serve.

Carrot, lentil and pasta soup

SERVES
4

INGREDIENTS

100 g (3½ oz) cresti di gallo
   pasta

1 tablespoon salt

1 tablespoon olive oil

1 carrot, roughly chopped

2 small onions, chopped

2 cloves garlic, crushed

½ tablespoon garam masala

200 g (7 oz) yellow lentils

8 cups (70 fl oz) vegetable
   stock

2 tablespoons chopped fresh
   coriander (cilantro)

METHOD

1. Place the pasta in lots of boiling water in a large
   saucepan with salt. Cook for 8 minutes or until just firm
   in the centre (al dente). Drain, set aside and keep warm.

2. Heat oil in a saucepan over a medium heat, add carrot,
   onions and garlic and cook, stirring occasionally, for
   10 minutes or until vegetables are soft. Add garam
   masala and cook, stirring, for 1 minute longer.

3. Add lentils and stock to pan and bring to the boil.
   Reduce heat and simmer, stirring occasionally, for
   30–40 minutes or until lentils are cooked. Cool slightly.

4. Purée the soup mixture, in batches, in a food processor
   or blender. Return the purée to a clean saucepan, add
   the pasta and cook over a low heat, stirring, for
   5 minutes or until soup is hot. Stir in cilantro and serve
   immediately.

Note

Cresti di gallo or 'cock's crests' is so named because it resembles a cock's comb.
About 3 cm (1 in) long, it's slightly curved, with a curly outer rib along the back.
Any small pasta shape suitable for soups, such as elbow (short-cut) pasta or
macaroni can be substituted.

Sweet Potato and Yam Soup

SERVES
6

INGREDIENTS

2 tablespoons butter

2 brown onions, diced

300 g (10½ oz) sweet potatoes, peeled and chopped

1½ kg (3 lb 5 oz) yams, roughly peeled and chopped

1 teaspoon ground nutmeg

1 teaspoon ground cardamom

8 cups (70 fl oz) vegetable or chicken stock

salt and freshly ground black pepper to taste

4 tablespoons sour cream

4 tablespoons yoghurt

extra nutmeg

1 small sweet potato, extra, finely sliced

1 tablespoon oil

1 teaspoon each of ground coriander (cilantro) and chilli powder

METHOD

1. Heat the butter in a large saucpan and add the diced onions. Cook the onions over a medium high heat for 5 minutes until they turn golden. Add the chopped sweet potatoes and yams and the nutmeg and cardamom and toss the vegetables together, coating them in the spices. Sauté for 10 minutes, stirring often.

2. Add the stock and bring the soup to the boil. Simmer for 40 minutes then purée the soup thoroughly. Season to taste with salt and pepper then return the soup to the saucepan.

3. Add the sour cream and yoghurt, then serve with spiced potato chips and a sprinkle of nutmeg.

4. To make the sweet potato chips, brush the finely sliced potato chips with a little oil then dust with combined ground coriander and chilli powder. Spread the sweet potato slices on baking paper and cook in the microwave on high until they are golden around the edges and tender, approximately 5 minutes.

Brussels sprout and leek soup

SERVES
6

INGREDIENTS

400 g (14 oz) Brussels
sprouts, trimmed

200 g (7 oz) white leek,
washed and trimmed

6 cups (50 fl oz) vegetable
stock

1 cup (9 fl oz) milk

50 g (1¾ oz) vermicelli,
broken

2 sprigs chervil, chopped

METHOD

1. Cut the sprouts into quarters or even more if they are
large. Slice the leeks very finely, crosswise. Place the two
ingredients into a boiling pot and pour in the stock.
Bring to the boil and cook until the sprouts are tender.

2. Add the milk and vermicelli and simmer for as long as it
takes to cook the vermicelli.

3. A few minutes before you are to serve, add the chervil.
Serve hot with hot wholemeal crusty bread and butter.

Spiced Pumpkin, Parsnip and Pear Soup with Lentil Crisps

SERVES
6-8

SOUP

1½ kg (3 lb 5 oz) pumpkin of your choice

1 tablespoon olive oil

500 g (1 lb 2 oz) parsnip, peeled and diced

2 small brown pears, peeled and diced

1 large Spanish onion, chopped

3 cloves garlic, minced

1 tablespoon curry powder

salt and pepper to taste

6-8 cups (50-70 fl oz) vegetable or chicken stock

½ cup (4 fl oz) dry white wine

½ cup (4 fl oz) low fat yoghurt or buttermilk

1 bunch chives, snipped

LENTIL CRISPS

½ cup (4½ oz) lentil flour

½ cup (4½ oz) plain flour

½ cup (4½ oz) semolina flour

¾ teaspoon curry powder

½ teaspoon salt

½ teaspoon pepper

2/3 cup (approx.) warm water

olive oil spray

METHOD

1. Cut the pumpkin in half and place in a baking tray with ½ cup (4 fl oz) of water and bake at 190°C (374°F) for 90 mins or until pumpkin is soft. Scoop out and discard seeds and peel off skin.

2. Heat the olive oil in a large saucepan and add diced parsnip, pears, chopped onions, garlic, curry powder and salt and pepper, sauté stirring occasionally for 20 mins. Add the cooked pumpkin, stock and white wine and bring to the boil.

3. Simmer uncovered for 40 mins then purée soup until smooth.

4. To serve, drizzle some buttermilk or yoghurt over the soup and scatter the chives on top. Place a lentil crisp across each bowl.

LENTIL CRISPS:

Preheat your oven to 220°C (428° F). In a bowl mix all the dry ingredients, salt and pepper and add enough of the water to form a kneadable dough. Knead for 2 mins then roll out as thinly as possible (or with pasta machine) to a rectangle of approx. 40 cm x 15 cm (15 in x 6 in). Using a knife, cut the dough into long, thin triangles and place on a non-stick tray. Spray with olive oil, add salt if desired and bake for 10 mins until crisp and golden. Cool on a wire rack and repeat with remaining dough.

Cream of cauliflower soup

SERVES
8

INGREDIENTS

750 g (1lb 10oz) cauliflower florets

200 g (7 oz) onions, chopped

6 cups (50 fl oz) chicken stock

6 cups (50 fl oz) milk

2 teaspoons salt

¼ teaspoon cayenne pepper

½ cup thickened cream

¼ cup parsley, chopped

METHOD

1. Combine the cauliflower, onions, stock and milk in a large boiling pot. Cook until the cauliflower is broken down. Remove from heat.

2. Blend the cauliflower and liquid, then return to the pot.

3. Season with salt and cayenne pepper, then add the cream. Reheat and serve garnished with chopped parsley.

Cream of vegetable soup

SERVES
6

INGREDIENTS

60 g (2 oz) butter

750 g (1 lb 10 oz)
prepared vegetables
(see below)

2 cups (17 fl oz) chicken
stock

salt and freshly ground
black pepper

½ cup thickened cream

¼ cup parsley, chopped

PUMPKIN AND LEEK

500 g (1 lb 2 oz)
pumpkin, peeled and
chopped

2 leeks, thinly sliced

¼ cup (4 fl oz) dry
sherry

VARIATIONS

750 g (1 lb 10 oz)
carrots, peeled and
roughly chopped,

½ teaspoon allspice OR
750 g (1 lb 10 oz)
broccoli, divided into
florets, ½ teaspoon
nutmeg OR

750 g (1 lb 10oz)
zucchini (courgette),
sliced, ¼ teaspoon
basil OR

750 g (1 lb 10 oz)
asparagus, ends
broken off, stems cut
in half OR

750 g (1 lb 10 oz)
mushrooms, washed
and sliced, ½ teaspoon
oregano, garnish
with thinly sliced
mushrooms

METHOD

1. Melt the butter in a saucepan,
   add vegetables and cook for
   10 minutes over medium heat.

2. Add stock and seasonings and
   simmer over low heat until
   vegetables are tender. Purée
   mixture.

3. Stir in cream and reheat without
   boiling. Garnish with parsley and
   serve immediately.

Cheese and onion soup

SERVES
6

INGREDIENTS

60 g (2¼ oz) butter

3 medium onions, finely diced

3 tablespoons plain (all-purpose) flour

salt and freshly ground black pepper

½ teaspoon paprika

¼ teaspoon sage

pinch of cayenne pepper

3 cups (25 fl oz) milk

1 cup (9 fl oz) thickened cream

160g (5½ oz) Cheddar cheese, grated

½ teaspoon Worcestershire sauce

3 drops Tabasco sauce

METHOD

1. Melt butter in a saucepan over a medium heat, add onions and sauté until tender. Add flour, spices and seasonings and cook for 3 minutes.

2. Gradually add milk and cream and cook, stirring continuously over a low heat until thick and smooth. Add cheese and stir until melted. Season with Worcestershire sauce and Tabasco.

Tomato soup

SERVES
4

INGREDIENTS

750 g (1 lb 10 oz) ripe
   tomatoes, chopped

1 potato, peeled and
   chopped

1 small onion, chopped

2 sprigs fresh basil

1 teaspoon sugar

2 tablespoons tomato paste

salt and freshly ground black
   pepper

1 cup (9 fl oz) vegetable
   stock

METHOD

1. Place all ingredients into a saucepan with the stock.
   Bring to the boil and simmer, covered, for 20 minutes.

2. Purée mixture.

3. Garnish with fresh basil and pepper.

Spinach, Tomato and Rocket Soup

SERVES 6

INGREDIENTS

2 tablespoons olive oil

2 onions, cut into fine dice

1 bunch rocket (arugula)

250 g (9 oz) fresh spinach, stemmed

2 tablespoons flour

1 litre (35 fl oz) vegetable stock

2 tablespoons lemon juice

1 kg (2 lb 4 oz) ripe tomatoes, diced

3 eggs

1 cup (9 fl oz) sour cream

200 g (7 oz) baby spinach leaves

salt and pepper to taste

several perfect rocket leaves to garnish

½ bunch chives

METHOD

1. Heat the olive oil in a large saucepan and add the onions. Cook over a high heat until golden and soft, about 5 minutes. Add the torn rocket and spinach and sauté until wilted. Sprinkle the flour over the vegetables and stir to combine. Cook for another 2 minutes, then gradually add stock and lemon juice while stirring to incorporate. Add the tomatoes and simmer for 20 minutes.

2. Break the eggs into a bowl and whisk briefly. Remove the soup from the heat and when it stops bubbling add the eggs and stir vigorously to distribute. When the soup appears more opaque (about 3 minutes), return the soup to the heat and simmer for 5 minutes.

3. Place the sour cream in a bowl and add a ladle of soup. Mix thoroughly then return to the soup.

4. Add the baby spinach and stir through without boiling, season to taste with salt and pepper.

5. Garnish with a rocket leaf or two and a sprinkle of chives and serve.

Traditional French Onion Soup

SERVES
8

INGREDIENTS

8 large onions

100g (3½ oz) butter (or oil)

2 cloves garlic, minced

1½ tablespoons flour

1 tablespoon sugar

1 litre (35 fl oz) good quality beef stock

2-3 cups (70 fl oz) water

½ cup (4 fl oz) red wine

4 tablespoons sherry/port

salt and pepper to taste

8 rounds of bread

½ cup (4½ oz) grated Gruyère

½ cup (4½ oz) grated Parmesan

½ cup (4½ oz) finely chopped parsley

METHOD

1. Peel and slice the onions into rounds. Heat the butter (or oil) and sauté the garlic and onions until they are shiny and golden brown, about 15 minutes. Add the flour and stir to allow the flour to absorb the butter residue.

2. Add the sugar, beef stock, water and wine and bring to the boil then simmer for 45 minutes. Add the sherry and simmer 5 minutes more. Add salt and pepper to taste.

3. Grill the bread until golden. Meanwhile, mix the two cheeses and parsley in a bowl. Place a large tablespoon of cheese mixture on each round of grilled bread and grill until cheese is hot and bubbling.

4. Place one round of bread in each soup bowl and then ladle boiling soup over. The crouton will rise to the top of the bowl, serve immediately.

Minestrone

SERVES
6

INGREDIENTS

⅓ cup (3 fl oz) olive oil

1 medium brown onion, sliced

1 clove garlic, crushed

250 g (9 oz) potatoes, peeled and chopped

150 g (5 oz) carrots, thinly sliced

125 g (4 oz) celery, thinly sliced

150 g (5 oz) zucchini (courgette), sliced

4 cups (35 fl oz) vegetable stock

400 g (14 oz) canned Roma tomatoes

rind from piece of Parmesan cheese

¼ cup parsley, chopped

400 g (14 oz) canned cannellini beans

salt and freshly ground black pepper

METHOD

1. Heat the oil in a saucepan and cook the onion and garlic for 5 minutes until onion is tender. Add the potatoes and cook for a further 5 minutes. Repeat with the carrots, celery and courgette.

2. Add the beef stock, tomatoes and cheese rind, bring to the boil and simmer covered for 1 hour. If the soup becomes too thick, add more stock.

3. Add the chopped parsley and cannellini beans, and heat for a further 10 minutes.

4. To serve, remove the cheese rind, season with salt and black pepper, and serve with crusty bread.

Spring cream soup

SERVES
8

INGREDIENTS

90 g (3 oz) butter

½ head celery, chopped

1 leek, sliced

2 carrots, peeled and
chopped

2 egg yolks

20 g (²/3 oz) Parmesan
cheese, grated

1 cup (9 fl oz) thickened
cream

¼ cup parsley, chopped

METHOD

1. In a large saucepan, melt butter over a low heat. Add vegetables and, stirring occasionally, cook gently until leek is transparent. Add 2 cups (17 fl oz) water, cover and simmer gently until vegetables are tender. Purée.

2. Combine the egg yolks, Parmesan and cream. Gradually stir egg mixture into soup and heat gently over a low heat without boiling. Garnish with parsley and serve.

Brown onion and egg yolk soup

SERVES
6

INGREDIENTS

50 g (1¾ oz) butter

600 g (1 lb 5 oz) onions, peeled and sliced

8 cups (70 fl oz) beef stock

¼ cup parsley, chopped

1 teaspoon salt

good pinch of cayenne pepper

nutmeg to taste

3 egg yolks

¼ cup (2 fl oz) port

METHOD

1. Melt the butter in a heavy-based saucepan and add the onions when the butter is foaming. Allow the onions to go a dark brown colour without burning. Stir the onions constantly while they are browning.

2. Add the stock and bring to the boil. Boil for 45 minutes and then add the parsley, salt and cayenne pepper and nutmeg. Bring back to the boil and cook for a further 10 minutes.

3. To serve, pour the soup into a tureen and keep hot. Take it to the table with the egg yolks and port wine already mixed in a sauceboat. Pour the egg yolk mixture into the soup while stirring and serve immediately with crusty bread.

Spicy Red Lentil and Pumpkin Soup

SERVES 6-8

INGREDIENTS

375 g (13 oz) red lentils

1 tablespoon olive oil

1 brown onion, finely chopped

2 cloves garlic, crushed

3 teaspoons ground cumin

2 teaspoons ground coriander (cilantro)

½ teaspoon chilli powder

½ teaspoon turmeric

1½ kg (3 lb 5 oz) butternut pumpkin, peeled, deseeded, and cut into 1cm (¼ in) pieces

6½ cups (57 fl oz) vegetable stock

salt and freshly ground black pepper

chilli flakes for garnish

METHOD

1. Place the lentils in a sieve and rinse under cold running water.

2. Heat the oil in a large heavy-based saucepan over medium-high heat. Add the onion and cook, stirring often, for 5 minutes or until it softens. Add the garlic, cumin, coriander, chilli powder and turmeric. Cook, stirring, for 30 seconds or until aromatic.

3. Add the lentils and stir to coat in the onion mixture. Stir in the pumpkin and stock. Increase heat to high and bring to the boil. Reduce heat to medium-low and simmer, covered, stirring often, for 15 minutes or until pumpkin and lentils are very soft.

4. Taste and season with salt and pepper. Garnish with chilli flakes to serve.

Couscous and Lentil Herb Soup

SERVES
4

INGREDIENTS

2 tablespoons peanut oil

4 cloves garlic, minced

2 fresh (or dried) bay leaves

1 large onion, roughly diced

1 tablespoon ground cumin

1 tablespoon ground coriander (cilantro)

1 teaspoon ground cloves

1 teaspoon ground cinnamon

1 teaspoon turmeric

5 cups (44 fl oz) vegetable stock

1 cup (9 oz) red lentils

1 cup (9 oz) couscous

½ cup chopped parsley

2 tablespoons chopped coriander (cilantro)

juice of 1 lemon

cracked black pepper

METHOD

1. Heat the peanut oil and add the minced garlic, bay leaves and the diced onion and sauté for 5 minutes or until the garlic is very brown and the onion is golden. Add all the spices and continue to cook until fragrant, about 2 minutes.

2. Add the stock and bring to the boil. Add the lentils and simmer for 1 hour or until they are tender.

3. Add the couscous and herbs and stir well. Turn off the heat and allow the soup to 'rest' for 5 minutes. Add a squeeze of lemon and lots of cracked pepper and serve immediately.

Cream of Asparagus and Basil

SERVES
6-8

INGREDIENTS

1 kg (2 lb 4 oz) fresh green
   asparagus

2 tablespoons butter

4 large shallots, finely
   chopped

20 basil leaves

6 tablespoons flour

pinch of saffron threads

6 cups (50 fl oz) chicken or
   vegetable stock

salt and freshly ground
   pepper to taste

2 egg yolks

1 cup (9 fl oz) full cream milk
   or light cream

peanut oil for frying

large basil leaves, extra

METHOD

1. Cut the tips off the asparagus and put in boiling water
   for 30 seconds. Drain and set aside. Cut the remaining
   stalks. Melt butter and sauté the asparagus stalks for
   2 mins. Add shallots and basil leaves and continue
   cooking for 5 mins or until vegetables soften.

2. Sprinkle flour over the vegetable mixture and stir
   through, making sure that all the flour is mixed in. Add
   saffron and chicken or vegetable stock and bring the
   mixture to the boil, stirring often.

3. Simmer for 20 mins or until the vegetables are tender.
   Purée the soup, either with a hand-held blender or food
   processor. Then return the soup to the saucepan and
   season to taste with salt and pepper.

4. Whisk the egg yolk and milk or cream together. Slowly
   add to the puréed soup, whisking constantly. Cook over
   low heat for 5 mins then check seasoning, adjusting with
   salt and pepper if necessary.

5. To Prepare the friend basil leaves, heat a little peanut oil
   then add a few basil leaves at a time (take care as leaves
   will split for a few seconds). Remove leaves as soon as
   they stop sizzling and drain them on paper towel.
   Repeat with remaining basil leaves.

6. Serve soup garnished with reserved asparagus tips,
   friend basil leaves and perhaps a little drizzle of cream
   if desired.

Pumpkin soup

SERVES
6

INGREDIENTS

1½ kg (3 lb 5 oz) pumpkin, peeled and cut into large cubes

2 tomatoes, chopped

1 large onion, chopped

5 cups (44 fl oz) vegetable stock

pinch of salt

pinch of cayenne pepper

⅔ cup thickened cream

¼ cup parsley, finely chopped

METHOD

1. Combine pumpkin, tomato and onions with the stock in a pan. Simmer gently until pumpkin is tender, approximately 20 minutes.

2. Purée pumpkin mixture. Return to pan, add salt, cayenne pepper and cream and reheat gently.

3. Serve sprinkled with parsley.

Savory Pumpkin Soup

SERVES
6-8

INGREDIENTS

1 kg (2 lb 2 oz) pumpkin,
    peeled, diced

400 ml (13 fl oz) canned
    tomato juice

1 tablespoon raw sugar

2 litres (70 fl oz) water

salt and freshly ground black
    pepper

1 bay leaf

few drops of Tabasco sauce

2 chicken stock cubes

125 ml (4 fl oz) pouring
    cream

2 tablespoons chopped fresh
    parsley

METHOD

1. With the exception of parsley and cream, combine all ingredients in a slow cooker and cook for 6½ hours on low.

2. Remove bay leaf. Process the mixture a cupful at a time in a food processor.

3. Return mixture to slow cooker and reheat for 15 minutes. Add cream and allow to warm through.

4. Serve sprinkled with fresh parsley.

Sweet Potato and Rosemary Soup

SERVES 6

INGREDIENTS

2 tablespoons olive oil

2 cloves garlic, crushed

1 medium onion, chopped

3 tablespoons chopped fresh rosemary

2 tablespoons puréed semi-dried tomato

1 medium carrot, sliced

1 large potato, sliced

700 g (1 lb 10 oz) sweet potato, sliced

1 litre (35 fl oz) chicken stock

salt and freshly ground black pepper

METHOD

1. Heat the oil in a saucepan, add the garlic, onion and one-third of the rosemary, and cook on a medium heat for 5 minutes. Add the semi-dried tomato purée and cook for 1 minute.

2. Add the carrot, potato and sweet potato, and cook for a further 6 minutes.

3. Transfer to the slow cooker set on high and add the stock and salt and pepper. Cook for 5 hours, or until the vegetables are soft.

4. Purée the soup in a food processor, then return to the slow cooker. Add the remaining rosemary and heat through before serving.

Chicken and Couscous Soup

SERVES
6

INGREDIENTS

1½ kg (3 lb 5 oz) chicken
   casserole pieces

400 g (14 oz) canned diced
   tomatoes

1 onion, coarsely grated

½ teaspoon ground cumin

½ teaspoon paprika

½ teaspoon turmeric

⅛ teaspoon Cayenne pepper
   or chilli powder

1 cinnamon stick

1 small clove garlic, crushed

salt and freshly ground black
   pepper

½ cup (4½ oz) couscous

½ cup mint, chopped

¼ cup flat-leaf parsley,
   chopped

¼ cup coriander (cilantro),
   chopped

2 teaspoons lemon juice

METHOD

1. Place the chicken pieces in a large saucepan and add
   the tomatoes, onion, cumin, paprika, turmeric, Cayenne
   or chilli, cinnamon, garlic, salt and pepper. Pour in
   3 cups (26 fl oz) of water, bring to the boil, reduce heat,
   cover and simmer gently for 45–50 minutes until chicken
   is tender.

2. Remove the chicken with a slotted spoon to a plate.
   Cool, then remove the bones and discard. Cut chicken
   meat into small pieces and return to saucepan.

3. Add 5 more cups (44 fl oz) of water and bring back to a
   simmer. Slowly add the couscous, stirring constantly to
   distribute evenly. Add the mint, parsley and coriander.
   Simmer uncovered for 10 minutes, stirring occasionally.
   Add lemon juice, adjust seasoning if needed and serve
   immediately.

Hot and sour soup

SERVES 6

INGREDIENTS

4 French shallots, sliced

2 fresh green chillies, chopped

6 kaffir lime leaves

4 slices fresh ginger

8 cups (70 fl oz) fish, chicken or vegetable stock

250 g (9 oz) firm fish fillets, cut into chunks

12 medium prawns (shrimp), shelled and deveined, tails left intact

12 mussels, scrubbed and beards removed

125 g (4 oz) oyster or straw mushrooms

3 tablespoons lime juice

2 tablespoons fish sauce

METHOD

1. Place the shallots, chillies, lime leaves, ginger and stock in a saucepan and bring to the boil over a high heat. Reduce the heat and simmer for 3 minutes.

2. Add the fish, prawns, mussels and mushrooms and cook for 3–5 minutes or until the fish and seafood are cooked. Discard any mussels that do not open after 5 minutes of cooking. Stir in the lime juice and fish sauce. To serve, ladle the soup into bowls, scatter with cilantro leaves and accompany with lime wedges.

Note

Straw mushrooms are one of the most popular mushrooms used in Asian cooking and in the West are readily available canned. Oyster mushrooms are also known as abalone mushrooms and range in colour from white to grey to pale pink. Their shape is similar to that of an oyster shell and they have a delicate flavour. Oyster mushrooms should not be eaten raw as some people are allergic to them in the uncooked state.

Hot and sour fish soup

SERVES
4-6

INGREDIENTS

1 kg (2 lb 4 oz) firm-fleshed
fish

1½ tablespoons nuoc cham
dipping sauce

¼ teaspoon white pepper

1 spring onion (scallion),
chopped

2 stalks lemongrass, bruised

55 g (2 oz) tamarind pulp

1 tablespoon sugar

250 g (9 oz) canned sliced
bamboo shoots

22 g (¾ oz) canned sliced
pineapple

2 tomatoes, cut into wedges

1 cup (9 oz) bean sprouts

¼ cup mixed fresh
Vietnamese herbs such as
cilantro (coriander), bitter
herb, Asian basil

deep-fried French shallots

METHOD

1. Remove head, fins and tail from fish and cut into 8–10
large pieces. Combine fish, nuoc cham, pepper and
spring onion, allow to marinate for 15 minutes.

2. Place 6 cups (50 fl oz) water in a large saucepan and
bring to the boil. Add the fish with its marinade and
lemongrass. Reduce heat and simmer for 20 minutes.

3. Meanwhile, combine tamarind pulp and ¾ cup boiling
water and allow to soak for 15 minutes. Strain mixture
through a fine sieve and discard pulp.

4. Add the tamarind liquid, sugar, bamboo shoots,
pineapple and tomatoes to the pan. Simmer for
4–5 minutes until fish is tender. Remove lemongrass.

5. Divide bean sprouts amongst serving bowls and spoon
hot soup over. Sprinkle with fresh herbs and deep-fried
shallots. Serve with lime wedges and sliced chilli on the
side.

Hot and sour chicken soup

SERVES
6

INGREDIENTS

600 g (21 oz) chicken breast
fillets, cut into 1 cm (¼ in)
thick strips

2 tablespoons peanut oil

4 cloves garlic, minced

2 French shallots, chopped

5 stems of coriander
(cilantro), leaves included,
chopped

30 g (1 oz) fresh ginger,
bruised

3 small red Thai chillies,
minced

3 stalks lemongrass, bruised

6 kaffir lime leaves, finely
shredded

8 cups (50 fl oz) chicken or
vegetable stock

3 tablespoons fish sauce

100 g (3½ oz) cellophane or
glass noodles

6 spring onions (scallions),
diagonally sliced

juice of 1–2 limes

½ cup coriander (cilantro)
leaves

METHOD

1. Brush the chicken strips with 1 tablespoon of peanut oil
and grill or pan-fry until the chicken is golden brown
and slightly charred, about 3 minutes each side.

2. Heat the remaining tablespoon of peanut oil in a large
saucepan and add the garlic, shallots, cilantro leaves
and stems, ginger, chillies, lemongrass and lime leaves
and toss in the hot oil until fragrant, about 2 minutes.
Add the stock and bring to the boil. Simmer for
10 minutes, then add the grilled chicken strips and
simmer for a further 10 minutes.

3. Add the fish sauce and noodles and simmer for a further
2 minutes, or until the noodles are tender. Add the
sliced scallions, lime juice and cilantro leaves, remove
the lemongrass and serve very hot.

Chicken and leek soup

SERVES
6

INGREDIENTS

1 kg (2 lb 4 oz) boiling chicken

1 onion, chopped

1 carrot, peeled and chopped

pinch saffron

1 stalk celery, chopped

2 leeks, finely sliced

30g (1 oz) butter

salt

cayenne pepper

½ cup (4 fl oz) thickened cream

METHOD

1. In a large pot, place the chicken, onion, carrot, saffron and celery. Cover the ingredients with water and boil for 1 hour.

2. Remove from the heat and strain off the stock. Reserve the chicken.

3. Sauté the leeks in the butter until soft, add the chicken stock and, heat through. Season with salt and cayenne pepper. Add cream as desired and serve.

Chicken and corn soup

SERVES
12

INGREDIENTS

1¼ kg (2 lb 12 oz) chicken

½ cup (4½ oz) water chestnuts, drained

1 small onion, peeled and halved

2 rashers bacon, each rasher cut into quarters, rind removed

1cm (¼ in) piece green ginger, peeled

440 g (15 oz) canned corn niblets, drained, reserving liquid

6 spring onions (scallions), sliced

2 teaspoons sesame oil

salt and freshly ground black pepper

3 tablespoons cornstarch (cornflour)

1 tablespoon sweet sherry

2 teaspoons soy sauce

1 egg

METHOD

1. Wash chicken and place into a large saucepan with 10 cups (88 fl oz) water. Bring to the boil and simmer approximately 40 minutes or until chicken is cooked. Remove chicken from pan, set aside to cool. Do not discard chicken stock. While chicken is cooking, prepare other ingredients.

2. Place water chestnuts, onion, bacon and ginger into food processor or blender bowl and process until finely chopped. Remove from bowl.

3. Purée corn niblets in food processor or blender.

4. Remove skin and bones from chicken. Place chicken into processor bowl and process until finely chopped.

5. Take 2 cups (17 fl oz) of chicken stock from pan and reserve for future use.

6. Add all prepared ingredients with reserved corn liquid to chicken stock.

7. Add green onions to saucepan with sesame oil, salt and pepper. Bring to boil. Mix cornstarch and ⅓ cup water to a smooth paste, add to soup and simmer, stirring, for 3 minutes. Add sherry and soy sauce. Lightly beat egg with a fork, add to soup and stir for 1 minute. Serve.

Chicken and coconut soup

SERVES
6

INGREDIENTS

3 cups (26 fl oz) coconut milk

500 g (17½ oz) chicken breast fillets, cut into 1 cm (¼ in) thick strips

4 cm (1½ in) piece fresh galangal or ginger, sliced

2 stalks lemongrass, cut into 4 cm (1½ in) pieces

1 fresh coriander (cilantro) root, bruised

4 kaffir lime leaves, shredded

3 fresh red chillies, deseeded and chopped

2 tablespoons fish sauce

2 tablespoons lemon juice

¼ cup fresh coriander (cilantro) leaves

METHOD

1. Place coconut milk and 2 cups (17 fl oz) water in a saucepan and bring to the boil over a medium heat. Add chicken, galangal or ginger, lemongrass, coriander root and lime leaves and simmer for 6 minutes.

2. Stir in chillies, fish sauce and lemon juice. To serve, ladle into bowls and scatter with coriander leaves.

Note

This popular Thai soup is known as Tom Kha Gai. When dining in the traditional Thai manner, soups are not served as a separate course but are eaten with the other dishes and rice.

Thai rice soup with chicken

SERVES
4

INGREDIENTS

½ cup (4½ oz) short-grain rice

1 tablespoon vegetable oil

1 large clove garlic, finely chopped

4 cm (1½ in) piece fresh ginger, finely grated

250 g (9 oz) chicken thigh or breast fillets, trimmed and diced

white pepper

2 tablespoons fish sauce

1 small onion, finely sliced

¼ cup fresh coriander (cilantro), chopped

1 spring onion (scallion), chopped

METHOD

1. Place rice in a large saucepan with 8 cups (70 fl oz) water and bring slowly to the boil. Simmer gently, adding more water as necessary so that mixture becomes a thin porridge consistency.

2. In a wok or large frying pan, heat the oil and stir-fry the garlic and ginger. Add the chicken and season with pepper and fish sauce. Add the onion and stir-fry until chicken is cooked, about 5 minutes. Stir into the rice stock.

3. Just before serving, stir in the cilantro and green onions. Ladle into heated bowls and garnish each with a few extra cilantro leaves, scallion and some sliced red chillies.

Tomato and meatball soup

SERVES
4

INGREDIENTS

1 egg, beaten

1 tablespoon soy sauce

1 tablespoon sherry

½ small onion, chopped

1 cm (¼ in) piece fresh ginger, finely grated

250 g (9 oz) lean minced pork or beef

2 tablespoons cornstarch (cornflour)

4 cups (35 fl oz) beef stock

1 leek, finely sliced

4 firm, ripe tomatoes, peeled, deseeded and diced

¼ cup fresh coriander (cilantro), chopped

METHOD

1. Combine the egg, soy sauce, sherry, onion and ginger in a bowl, add the meat and cornstarch, then mix well and set aside.

2. Place the stock in a large saucepan, add the leek and tomatoes and bring to the boil. Boil for 2–3 minutes, then lower the heat.

3. Drop rounded teaspoonfuls of the meat mixture into the soup, cover and gently simmer for 3–4 minutes or until meatballs are cooked. Serve sprinkled with cilantro.

Note

The meatballs for this soup are also delicious made with thyme, rosemary or parsley. Or you might like to try a mixture of herbs for something different.

Mulligatawny

SERVES 4

INGREDIENTS

30 g (1 oz) butter

1 small onion, finely diced

1 cm (¼ in) piece ginger, grated

1 tablespoon curry powder

1 tablespoon plain (all-purpose) flour

1 tablespoon desiccated coconut

4 cups (35 fl oz) chicken stock

1 bouquet garni

1 tablespoon tomato paste

1 tablespoon mango chutney

½ small banana, sliced

150 g (5½ oz) cooked chicken breast, diced

juice of ½ lemon

salt and freshly ground black pepper

1 sprig coriander

METHOD

1. Melt butter in a saucepan over medium heat. Add onion, ginger and curry powder and cook until onion is tender. Add the flour and coconut and cook for a further 2 minutes. Add the stock, bouquet garni and tomato paste. Bring to the boil and simmer over low heat for 45 minutes.

2. Add the chutney, banana, chicken, lemon juice and seasonings. Heat through, remove bouquet garni and serve sprinkled with boiled rice.

3. Sprinkle with chopped coriander.

Vermicelli and chicken soup

SERVES
6

INGREDIENTS

150 g (5½ oz) chicken breast,
cut into chunks

250 g (9 oz) Chinese mung
bean vermicelli

½ cup (4½ oz) button
mushrooms, sliced

salt

½ teaspoon black or white
pepper

1 spring onion (scallion),
chopped

STOCK

3 teaspoons fish sauce

1 onion, quartered

1½ kg (3 lb 5 oz) pork bones

500 g (17½ oz) chicken
wings, bones and/or
leftover meat scraps

500 g (17½ oz) of 2 of the
following: whole carrot,
quartered cauliflower,
whole green beans, quarter
of a cabbage

METHOD

1. Make stock by boiling all ingredients together with
   8 cups (70 fl oz) water, then simmering for 1 hour. Strain
   reduced stock and discard the bones and vegetables.

2. Boil chicken chunks in stock for 15 minutes, skimming
   scum from the surface. Add vermicelli and mushrooms,
   and cook until vermicelli is done.

3. Season with salt and pepper and serve sprinkled with
   chopped spring onion.

Chicken vegetable soup with cheese sticks

SERVES 6

INGREDIENTS

2 skinless chicken breast fillets

4 cups (35 fl oz) chicken stock

1 tablespoon canola oil

2 leeks, washed and thinly sliced

2 carrots, diced

$\frac{1}{3}$ cup (2¾ oz) barley

2 stalks celery, diced

3 cloves garlic, crushed

6 cups (50 fl oz) young green leaves (watercress, rocket, sorrel, baby spinach), washed

3 tablespoons fresh pesto

freshly cracked black pepper

CHEESE STICKS

1 sheet puff pastry, thawed

40 g (1½ oz) Cheddar cheese, finely grated

METHOD

1. Put the chicken in a pot, add just enough chicken stock to cover it and poach gently for about 10 minutes or until just cooked. Set aside to cool.

2. Heat the oil in a large pot, add the leeks and cook gently for about 2 minutes until soft. Add the carrot, celery, barley and garlic, strain the chicken poaching stock through a fine sieve and add to the vegetables with the rest of the stock. Simmer for 10 minutes. Chop the greens finely, add them to the soup and cook for a further 10 minutes.

3. Tear the chicken breasts into fine shreds and add them to the soup. Stir in the pesto and season with plenty of cracked black pepper.

CHEESE STICKS

4. Preheat the oven to 220°C (420°F). Cut the puff pastry into 2 cm (¾ in) thick strips and place on a baking tray lined with baking paper. Sprinkle with the cheese and bake for 20 minutes or until crisp and golden.

5. Serve the soup in wide bowls with cheese sticks.

Clam chowder

SERVES
6

INGREDIENTS

45 g (1½ oz) butter

3 rashers bacon, chopped

1 onion, chopped

1 stalk celery, chopped

1 carrot, chopped

1 potato, peeled and chopped

280 g (10 oz) canned clams, drained and chopped

3 tablespoons plain (all-purpose) flour

2½ cups (25 fl oz) milk

salt and freshly ground black pepper

1 tablespoon brandy

METHOD

1. Melt 15 g (½ oz) of butter in pan, add bacon and vegetables and cook gently until soft.

2. Add 1¼ cups (12½ fl oz) water and potatoes to vegetables. Simmer until vegetables are tender, approximately 15–20 minutes.

3. Add clams to vegetables and remove the pan from the heat.

4. Melt remaining butter in pan, stir in the flour and cook for 1 minute. Remove from heat and gradually stir in milk.

5. Return soup to heat and add milk mixture. Cook until soup boils and thickens, stirring constantly. Season with salt and pepper, stir through brandy and serve.

Fragrant Asian Seafood Soup

SERVES
6-8

INGREDIENTS

1½ litres (3 lb 5 oz) fish or vegetable stock (or a mix)

2 tablespoons kecap manis (Indonesian sweet soy)

2 tablespoons fish sauce

2 tablespoons mirin

2 tablespoons finely sliced ginger

4 baby bok choy

6 spring onions, both green and white parts

100 g (3½ oz) oyster mushrooms

100 g (3½ oz) fresh shiitake mushrooms (optional)

1 kg (2 lb 4 oz) fish or shellfish of your choice (I like prawns, calamari and salmon)

2 cups (1 lb 2 oz) steamed white rice

½ bunch coriander (cilantro)

METHOD

1. Heat the stock and, when simmering, add the kecap manis, fish sauce, mirin and ginger. Stir well.

2. Meanwhile, wash the bok choy very well and cut off the leaves and set them aside. Slice the crunchy white stems and set aside.

3. Chop the spring onions and add to the simmering broth then add the sliced oyster and shiitake mushrooms (if using). Add the shellfish and fish, trimmed and chopped to your liking, and simmer for 5 minutes.

4. Add the white bok choy stems and simmer for 2 more minutes. If you wish, the ginger can be removed at this stage (I like to leave it in).

5. Prepare each bowl by placing a scoop of rice in the centre and several bok choy leaves around. Ladle the simmering broth and other ingredients into each bowl and garnish with fresh coriander leaves.

6. Serve immediately.

Lebanese Saffron and Roasted Eggplant Soup

SERVES 6

INGREDIENTS

2 large eggplants

salt

a little olive oil

2 tablespoons olive oil, extra

1 white onion, chopped

6 shallots, chopped

6 spring onions, sliced

3 cloves garlic, minced

2 tablespoons fresh oregano

2 large potatoes, peeled and diced

8 cups (70 fl oz) chicken or vegetable stock

good pinch of saffron threads

½ cup (4 fl oz) yoghurt

1 teaspoon ground cumin

1 teaspoon ground coriander

2 tablespoons chives

METHOD

1. Cut the eggplants into thick slices and place them on a wire rack. Sprinkle generously with salt and allow to 'rest' for at least thirty minutes. Rinse briefly in cold water, dry well, then brush lightly with olive oil.

2. Grill the eggplant slices on both sides until golden. Meanwhile, heat the 2 tablespoons of olive oil and add the chopped onion, shallots, spring onions, garlic and oregano. Sauté until the onion mixture is soft then add the diced potato, continue to cook for 10 minutes.

3. Add the stock and saffron threads and simmer for 25 minutes until the potato is soft.

4. Meanwhile, mix the yoghurt with the spices and set aside.

5. Roughly chop the roasted eggplant and add to the soup and simmer for a further minute or two to allow the flavours to blend.

6. Season the soup with salt and pepper then purée the soup. Serve hot with a little spiced yoghurt and chives.

Curried fish soup

SERVES
8

INGREDIENTS

60 g (2¼ oz) butter

1 small leek, washed and thinly sliced

1 medium carrot, thinly sliced

1 small onion, chopped

1 tablespoon curry powder

1 tomato, peeled, seeds removed and chopped

2 cups (17 fl oz) fish stock

1 large potato, peeled and diced

1 teaspoon brown sugar

½ teaspoon salt

250 g (9 oz) fish fillets, cut into 25 mm (1 in) pieces

salt and freshly ground black pepper

1 cup (9 fl oz) thickened cream

¼ cup parsley, chopped

METHOD

1. Heat butter in a saucepan and sauté leek, carrot and onion over a low heat for 5 minutes or until the vegetables are tender.

2. Stir in curry powder and cook for 2 minutes. Add tomato and cook for 5 minutes. Stir in stock, potato, sugar and salt and bring to the boil. Reduce the heat and simmer for 15 minutes.

3. Add fish and seasonings and simmer for a further 10 minutes. Stir through cream and reheat without boiling. Sprinkle with parsley and serve.

Corn and smoked fish soup

SERVES
8

INGREDIENTS

300 g (10½ oz) smoked fish

8 cups (70 fl oz) fish stock

4 cobs of corn

salt

cayenne pepper

4 egg yolks

1 cup (9 fl oz) thickened
cream

8 sprigs of dill

METHOD

1. Poach the smoked fish in the fish stock for 5 minutes.
   You can add some white wine if you so desire.

2. Remove the fish from the stock and cool. Strip the corn
   husks then cut the corn kernels from the cob. Place the
   kernels into the stock and boil until they are tender.

3. Blend or process the stock with the kernels. Return to
   the pot and season with salt and cayenne pepper. Flake
   the fish, add to the soup and bring to the boil.

4. In a separate bowl, mix the egg yolks and the cream.
   Remove the soup from the heat and allow to cool a
   little. Add the egg yolks and cream, stirring all the time.

5. When ready to serve, bring up to a near boil. In no
   circumstances allow the soup to boil or it will curdle.
   Serve garnished with a sprig of dill.

Seafood dumpling soup

SERVES 8

INGREDIENTS

1 tablespoon olive oil

2 onions, finely chopped

750 g (1 lb 10 oz) minced white-fleshed fish

1 tablespoon anchovy sauce

1 egg, lightly beaten

½ teaspoon salt

½ teaspoon freshly ground black pepper

8 cups (70 fl oz) fish stock

2 green onion tops, chopped

METHOD

1. Heat the oil in a frying pan, add the onion and cook for 5 minutes. Place fish into a mixing bowl and add the onion, anchovy sauce, egg, salt and pepper. Mix well, mould into balls and set to one side.

2. Bring the fish stock to the boil and then simmer. Add the moulded fish balls to this stock. Simmer for 20 minutes.

3. Serve in a tureen, or in individual bowls, sprinkled with the green onion tops.

Spiced Fish, Tomato and Chickpea Soup

SERVES
6

INGREDIENTS

1 tablespoon olive oil

1 onion, chopped

1 teaspoon ground coriander (cilantro)

1 teaspoon ground cumin

1 teaspoon allspice

1 green chilli, finely sliced

400 g (14 oz) canned chopped tomatoes

400 g (14 oz) canned chickpeas, rinsed and drained

1 litre (35 fl oz) reduced-salt fish stock

500 g (1 lb 2 oz) firm white fish fillets such as redfish, bream or sea perch, cut into large pieces

⅓ cup (2¾ oz) couscous

½ cup (4 fl oz) natural yoghurt

¼ cup fresh parsley, chopped

¼ cup fresh mint, chopped

METHOD

1. Heat the oil in a large pot, add the onion and cook over a medium heat for 3 minutes or until soft and golden.

2. Add the spices and chilli and cook until fragrant, about 2 minutes. Stir in the tomatoes, chickpeas and fish stock and bring to the boil. Reduce the heat and simmer uncovered for 15 minutes.

3. Add the fish and cook for 5 minutes or until the fish is just tender. Remove the soup from the heat, then add the couscous and cover. Set aside for 10 minutes or until the couscous is soft.

4. Serve with a dollop of yoghurt and sprinkled with parsley and mint.

Mexican Chicken Soup

SERVES
10

INGREDIENTS

10 cups (88 fl oz) chicken stock

2 sprigs thyme

1 head (bulb) of garlic, unpeeled

2 fresh (or bottled) jalapeño chillies

3 large tomatoes, diced

2 medium onions

500 g (1 lb 2 oz) cooked chicken meat

½ cup chopped coriander (cilantro)

½ cup chopped parsley

2 ripe avocados

100 g (3 /2 oz) sour cream

juice of 1 lime

METHOD

1. Heat the broth to a simmer with the thyme sprigs and head of garlic, sliced in half horizontally (but not peeled). Simmer for 1 hour. Meanwhile, cut the jalapeño chillies in half and discard the seeds. Mince the chilli and set aside. Dice the tomatoes and onions. Shred the cooked chicken meat.

2. After the soup has simmered for an hour, remove the garlic and thyme sprigs and add the chilli, tomatoes and onions and simmer for a further 10 minutes. Add the shredded chicken meat and simmer for a further minute, then add salt and pepper to taste.

3. To serve, stir through the coriander and parsley then top the soup with finely diced avocado, a dollop of sour cream and a few drops of lime juice.

Carrot, Almond and Sour Cream Soup

SERVES
6

INGREDIENTS

2 tablespoons butter

100 g (3½ oz) blanched whole almonds

2 medium onions, diced

4 cloves garlic, minced

1 tablespoon fresh minced ginger

1-2 small red chillies, minced

1 kg (2 lb 4 oz) medium carrots, peeled and sliced

3 teaspoons turmeric

3 teaspoons ground coriander (cilantro)

4 cups (35 fl oz) vegetable stock

1 cup (9 fl oz) sour cream

1 cup (9 fl oz) plain yoghurt

salt and pepper to taste

1 bunch chives

50 g (1¾ oz) toasted flaked almonds

METHOD

1. Melt the butter in a large saucepan and add the almonds and toast for a minute or two until golden. Add the onion, garlic, ginger and chillies and sauté until the onions are golden brown, about 5 minutes.

2. Add the carrots, turmeric and ground coriander and sauté for a further 10 minutes, stirring often.

3. Add the stock and bring the soup to the boil. Simmer for 30 minutes then add the sour cream and yoghurt. Purée the soup, adding salt and pepper to taste.

4. Reheat gently but do not allow to boil. Serve with plenty of snipped chives and some flaked toasted almonds.

Seafood bisque

SERVES
8

INGREDIENTS

90 g (3 oz) butter

1 small onion, diced

1 clove garlic, crushed

1 small carrot, diced

1 stalk celery, sliced

3 cups (26 fl oz) fish stock

2 tablespoons lemon juice

1 bay leaf

1 sprig thyme, leaves
removed and stalks
discarded

¼ teaspoon Tabasco sauce

¼ teaspoon Worcestershire
sauce

1 cup (9 fl oz) thickened
cream

1 kg (2 lb 4 oz) seafood,
finely diced

½ cup (4 fl oz) dry white wine

1 lemon, thinly sliced

¼ cup parsley, chopped

METHOD

1. Melt butter and sauté onion and garlic for 5 minutes.
   Add carrot and celery and cook for a further 3 minutes.

2. Combine the fish stock, lemon juice, bay leaf, thyme,
   Tabasco and Worcestershire sauce, add to the pot and
   simmer for 30 minutes or until vegetables are tender.

3. Remove bay leaf, purée mixture, add cream, seafood and
   wine and reheat without boiling.

Mussel soup in roasted tomato sauce

SERVES
6

INGREDIENTS

1½ kg (3 lb 5 oz) mussels

400 g (14 oz) fresh tomatoes, halved

⅓ cup olive oil

4 cloves garlic, crushed

1 brown onion, chopped

100 ml (3½ fl oz) white wine

400 g (14 oz) canned peeled tomatoes

¼ cup tomato paste

100 ml (3½ fl oz) fish stock

10 sprigs fresh oregano, leaves removed and chopped

salt and freshly ground black pepper

METHOD

1. Preheat the oven to 180°C (350°F). Wash mussels under water, scrub the shells with a scourer, and remove their beards. Discard any mussels that are open.

2. Place halved fresh tomatoes on a baking tray, drizzle with olive oil, sprinkle with salt and roast in the oven for 20 minutes.

3. Heat a little oil in a saucepan and sauté the garlic and the onion until soft. Add the white wine and cook for 2 minutes. Add the roasted tomatoes, canned tomatoes, tomato paste, stock and chopped oregano. Simmer for 5–10 minutes. Season with salt and pepper. Add mussels, cover, and cook for a further 5 minutes, until mussels have opened. Discard any that do not open.

4. Serve with crusty Italian bread.

Mussel and shrimp soup

SERVES
6

INGREDIENTS

1 kg (2 lb 4 oz) fresh mussels

500 g (17½ oz) cooked king
 prawns (shrimp)

1 large onion, chopped

2 stalks celery, chopped

2 large carrots, chopped

¼ cup parsley, chopped

8 cups (70 fl oz) fish stock

2 cups (17 fl oz) white wine

3 French shallots, chopped

1¼ cups (11 fl oz) thickened
 cream

salt and freshly ground
 black pepper

METHOD

1. Scrub and remove beards from mussels. Soak in clean water for at least 3 hours before use. Peel prawns, place the heads and shells into a boiling pot. Reserve the peeled shrimp for another meal or deep freeze for another occasion.

2. Add the onion, celery, carrot, parsley, fish stock and white wine to the pot. Bring to the boil and then simmer for 45 minutes. Strain the prawn stock.

3. Place the mussels in a suitable size pot, pour in the stock and add the shallots. Boil for 20 minutes. If you need more liquid, add some white wine. Before serving, add the cream and check seasoning. Serve with fresh crusty bread.

Prawn (Shrimp) and pasta soup

SERVES
6

INGREDIENTS

1½ kg (3 lb 5 oz) cooked prawns (shrimp)

1 small onion, chopped

1 stalk celery, chopped

1 small carrot, chopped

300 g (10½ oz) pasta of choice

2 tablespoons olive oil

4 large cloves garlic, chopped

4 sprigs fresh oregano, leaves removed and chopped

1 large sprig basil, chopped

400 g (14 oz) canned chopped tomatoes

2 tablespoons tomato paste

1 teaspoon salt

1 teaspoon freshly ground black pepper

½ cup (4 fl oz) dry vermouth

METHOD

1. Peel the shrimp, place the heads and shells into a boiling pot, add the onion, celery and carrot. Cover with 6 cups (50 fl oz) water and boil for 20 minutes, then strain. Reserve the stock and make sure you push all the juice from the heads with the back of a wooden spoon. Discard the solids.

2. Bring a large saucepan of salted water to the boil, add the pasta and cook for 8 minutes or until just firm in the centre (al dente). Drain, set aside and keep warm.

3. In a saucepan, heat the oil, add all remaining ingredients except the prawns and cook for 5 minutes. Add the stock and boil for a further 15 minutes. Reduce the heat, add the prawns and cook for 3 minutes.

4. Reheat the pasta by pan frying or running under hot water. Divide between six soup bowls and ladle the soup into the bowls. Serve with crusty bread.

Moroccan Chickpea Lentil Soup

SERVES
10

INGREDIENTS

1 medium onion, sliced

2 stalks celery, chopped

3 cloves garlic, crushed

1 red capsicum (bell pepper), diced

2 teaspoons olive oil

½ teaspoon ground cinnamon

½ teaspoon ground ginger

½ teaspoon turmeric

6 cups (50 fl oz) vegetable stock

⅓ cup lentils, rinsed

2 x 400 g (14 oz) canned chickpeas, drained and rinsed

400 g (14 oz) canned chopped tomatoes

¼ cup lemon juice

½ cup coriander (cilantro), finely chopped

salt and freshly ground black pepper

METHOD

1. Sauté onion, celery, garlic and capsicum in the oil until softened. Add cinnamon, ginger and turmeric.

2. Stirring thoroughly, add stock and lentils and bring to the boil. Reduce heat, cover and simmer for 45 minutes.

3. Add chickpeas and tomatoes and cook for another 15 minutes. Stir in lemon juice, coriander and salt and pepper to taste. Serve immediately.

Pork, mushroom and corn soup

SERVES
4

INGREDIENTS

200 g (7 oz) lean pork

4 dried Chinese mushrooms

425 g (15 oz) canned baby
corn

1 tablespoon oil

2 cloves garlic, crushed

½ teaspoon ground black
pepper

1 coriander (cilantro) plant,
roots included, chopped

1 onion, chopped

2 tablespoons fish sauce

½ cup fresh basil, chopped

METHOD

1. Chop pork and set aside. Soak dried mushrooms in boiling water for 30 minutes. Drain and slice. Drain baby corn and rinse well, then cut into bite-size pieces.

2. Meanwhile, heat oil in a large saucepan, add garlic, pepper, cilantro and onion and fry for 2 minutes. Add chopped pork and fry until pork is golden brown.

3. Add 4 cups (35 fl oz) water, fish sauce, baby corn and mushrooms and bring to the boil. Lower heat, cover and simmer for 10 minutes. Serve hot, sprinkled with chopped basil leaves.

Broccoli and bacon soup

SERVES 4

INGREDIENTS

1 tablespoon olive oil

1 large onion, roughly chopped

2 cloves garlic, chopped

3 cups (26 fl oz) chicken stock

500 g (17½ oz) broccoli

3 rashers bacon, rind removed, cut into small pieces

1 cup (9 fl oz) milk

freshly ground black pepper

METHOD

1. Heat the oil in a large saucepan and sauté the onion and garlic for 5 minutes until clear. Pour in stock and bring to the boil.

2. Add broccoli and cook for 10 minutes until just tender. Purée in a blender or food processor.

3. Return soup to saucepan. Mix in bacon and milk. Cook for 5 minutes. Season with freshly ground black pepper. Serve garnished with chopped chives.

Long soup

SERVES 12

INGREDIENTS

¼ cup water chestnuts, drained

1 cm (¼ in) cube green ginger

125 g (4 oz) bamboo shoots, drained

125 g (4 oz) lean pork, cut into 25 mm (1 in) cubes

1 tablespoon oil

250 g (9 oz) cabbage, sliced

5 spring onions (scallions), sliced

2 slices ham

12 cups (105½ fl oz) chicken stock

salt and freshly ground black pepper

¼ cup (2 fl oz) soy sauce

90 g (3 oz) thin egg noodles

¼ cup (2 fl oz) sweet sherry

METHOD

1. Place ham, water chestnuts, ginger and bamboo shoots into food processor bowl. Process until finely chopped. Set aside.

2. Finely mince one-third of the cubed pork at a time. Heat oil in a large saucepan, add minced pork and cook for 5 minutes, stirring frequently. Add the cabbage, scallions, ham, water chestnuts, ginger, bamboo shoots, stock, salt, pepper, soy sauce and egg noodles. Bring to boil and simmer for 10 minutes or until noodles are tender. Stir through sherry and serve.

Stone soup

SERVES
4–6

INGREDIENTS

1 tablespoon olive oil

1 onion, finely chopped

2 cloves garlic, crushed

200 g (7 oz) smoked bacon, diced

250 g (9 oz) smoked ham hock or bacon bones

2 potatoes, diced

2 carrots, diced

2 turnips, diced

2 stalks celery, diced

2 bay leaves

6 cups (50 fl oz) vegetable or chicken stock

150 g (5 oz) Savoy or green cabbage, shredded

400 g (14 oz) canned red kidney beans, drained and rinsed

¼ cup fresh parsley, chopped

salt and freshly ground black pepper

METHOD

1. Heat the oil in a large saucepan over medium heat. Cook the onion and garlic until soft. Add the bacon and cook for 2 minutes. Add the ham hock or bacon bones, potatoes, carrots, turnips, celery, bay leaves and stock.

2. Bring to the boil, reduce heat to low and simmer covered for 40–45 minutes or until vegetables are tender. If time permits, simmer for 1 hour, as this gives the soup more flavour. Add cabbage and kidney beans and simmer for a further 5 minutes.

3. Remove ham hock or bacon bones and cut the meat into small pieces. Return meat to the saucepan, add parsley and season with salt and pepper. Serve with crusty bread.

Pea soup

SERVES
8

INGREDIENTS

250 g (9 oz) split peas

500 g (17½ oz) bacon bones

2 carrots, roughly chopped

2 turnips, roughly chopped

2 onions, roughly chopped

4 stalks celery, chopped

salt and freshly ground
black pepper

1 tablespoon plain (all-
purpose) flour, mixed with
1 tablespoon water

METHOD

1. Wash peas and soak in water overnight. Place peas, water and bones in a saucepan and bring to the boil. Add prepared vegetables and simmer for 1½ hours.

2. Remove bones, purée mixture, and season with salt and pepper. Thicken with flour paste and, stirring continuously, cook for 3 minutes. Garnish with croutons and serve immediately.

Oxtail and tomato soup

SERVES
6

INGREDIENTS

1 medium oxtail

1 medium onion, chopped

1 large carrot, sliced

1 stalk celery, diced

8 cups (70 fl oz) beef stock

2 tomatoes, peeled,
    deseeded and chopped

salt and freshly ground
    black pepper

1 sprig rosemary, leaves
    removed and chopped

METHOD

1. Have the oxtail cut into sections by your butcher and place it in a boiling pot with the onion, carrot, celery and beef stock.

2. Simmer until the meat is cooked and is leaving the bone. Remove from the heat and lift the oxtail out. Reserve the stock. Cool the meat and then remove it from the bone. Dice finely and return it to the reserved stock.

3. Add the tomato, rosemary, salt and pepper. Bring to the boil and cook for 10 minutes. Check the seasoning and serve with crusty bread.

Chicken soup with lemon and mint

SERVES
4

INGREDIENTS

1 tablespoon olive oil

500 g (17½ oz) chicken breast fillets, trimmed

8 cups (70 fl oz) chicken stock

¾ cup (6½ oz) medium- or long-grain rice

¼ cup (2 fl oz) lemon juice

⅓ cup fresh mint, chopped

salt and freshly ground black pepper

METHOD

1. Heat oil in a large saucepan over medium heat. Add chicken fillets and cook for 2 minutes each side or until just light golden. Add ½ cup (4 fl oz) stock and simmer over low heat until chicken is cooked. Remove and cut into thin slices.

2. Heat remaining stock in saucepan over medium heat. Bring to the boil, add rice and cook for 12 minutes or until cooked. Add chicken and cook for a further 5 minutes.

3. Stir in lemon juice, mint and season to taste with salt and pepper. Serve with crusty bread.

Pork soup

SERVES
4

INGREDIENTS

1 tablespoon olive oil

1 medium onion, chopped

½ green capsicum (bell
pepper), chopped

4 large cloves garlic, minced

1 jalapeño pepper, deseeded
and minced

500 g (17½ oz) pork
tenderloin, trimmed and
cut into bite-size pieces

2 cups (17 fl oz) chicken
stock

2 teaspoons chilli powder

1 teaspoon ground cumin

½ teaspoon salt

¼ teaspoon black pepper

500 g (17½ oz) canned pinto
beans, rinsed and drained

400 g (14 oz) canned diced
tomatoes, undrained

¼ cup fresh coriander
(cilantro), chopped

1 avocado, diced

METHOD

1. Heat a small non-stick casserole dish over medium-heat
   and add oil.

2. Add onion, capsicum, garlic and jalapeño and sauté for
   2 minutes.

3. Add pork and cook for 3 minutes. Add stock, chilli
   powder, cumin, salt, pepper, pinto beans and tomatoes
   and bring to the boil.

4. Partially cover, reduce heat, and simmer for 6 minutes or
   until pork is done, stirring occasionally. Remove from
   heat and stir in cilantro. Serve with avocado.

Asian pork soup

SERVES 4

INGREDIENTS

2 tablespoons olive oil

400 g (14 oz) pork fillet, cut into thin bite-size pieces

100 g (3½ oz) shiitake mushrooms, sliced

2 cloves garlic, minced

6 cups (50 fl oz) chicken stock

2 tablespoons dry sherry

2 tablespoons soy sauce

2 cm (¾ in) piece ginger, minced

¼ teaspoon red pepper

150 g (5 oz) Chinese cabbage, thinly sliced

1 spring onion (scallion), thinly sliced

METHOD

1. Heat the oil in a large non-stick saucepan over medium heat. Add pork to hot saucepan and cook for 2–3 minutes or until slightly pink in centre.

2. Remove from the saucepan and set aside. Add mushrooms and garlic to saucepan and stir until tender over medium heat.

3. Stir in chicken stock, sherry, soy sauce, ginger, and red pepper. Bring to the boil. Stir in pork, Chinese cabbage, and green onion, heat through and serve.

Corn and bacon chowder

SERVES
8

INGREDIENTS

6 rashers bacon, rind
removed, chopped

1 medium onion, thinly sliced

500 g (17½ oz) potatoes,
peeled and medium diced

880 g (29½ oz) canned
creamed sweetcorn

3 cups (26 fl oz) milk

1 sprig thyme, leaves
removed and stalk
discarded

salt and freshly ground
black pepper

dash of Worcestershire sauce

METHOD

1. Place bacon in a saucepan and sautè over medium heat
until crisp. Remove and drain on absorbent paper.

2. Sautè onion until tender, add potatoes and 5 cups
(44 fl oz) boiling water and cook for a further 10 minutes.
Add sweetcorn, milk, thyme and bacon,
bring to the boil, season with salt, pepper and
Worcestershire sauce. Garnish with extra fresh thyme or
fresh sage.

Heavenly soup with ham

SERVES
4

INGREDIENTS

4 cups (35 fl oz) chicken stock

1½ tablespoons light soy sauce

1 teaspoon sugar

2 eggs, lightly beaten

1 slice of ham, finely diced

2 spring onions (scallions), finely chopped

METHOD

1. Bring stock to the boil, and add soy sauce and sugar.

2. Just before serving, pour the eggs into the stock, but do not stir. The egg should soon coagulate into egg flowerets. Stir only when the egg has started to set. Garnish with ham and scallions and serve.

Chunky lamb soup

SERVES
6

INGREDIENTS

30 g (1 oz) butter

500 g (17½ oz) lamb fillet,
 cut into ¾in (2cm) cubes

1 large onion, chopped

¼ cup fresh parsley, chopped

2 teaspoons paprika

1 teaspoon saffron powder

1 teaspoon freshly ground
 black pepper

6 cups lamb or chicken stock

60 g (2 oz) chickpeas, soaked
 overnight in water

500 g (17½ oz) tomatoes,
 peeled, deseeded and
 chopped

4 tablespoons lemon juice

60 g (2 oz) long-grain rice

METHOD

1. Melt the butter in a large saucepan over moderate heat.
 Add lamb cubes, onion, parsley, paprika, saffron and
 pepper. Cook for 5 minutes, stirring frequently.

2. Add the stock. Drain chickpeas and add them to pan
 with tomatoes and lemon juice. Bring to the boil,
 boil for 10 minutes, then cover pan and simmer fo
 1–1¼ hours.

3. Stir in rice. Cook for 15–20 minutes or until tender.
 Serve at once, in heated bowls.

Lamb shank and vegetable soup

SERVES
6

INGREDIENTS

4 lamb shanks, French
trimmed

3 stalks celery, cut into 1 cm
(¼ in) pieces

2 medium carrots, peeled
and cut into 1 cm (¼ in)
pieces

1 swede, peeled and cut into
1 cm (¼ in) cubes

1 parsnip, peeled and cut
into 1 cm (¼ in) cubes

800 g (1 lb 12 oz) canned
tomato soup

⅓ cup flat-leaf parsley,
coarsely chopped

salt and freshly ground
black pepper

METHOD

1. Combine lamb shanks, celery, carrot, swede, parsnip,
tomato soup and 6 cups (50 fl oz) cold water in a large
saucepan over high heat and bring to the boil. Reduce
heat to low and simmer, covered, stirring occasionally,
for 2¼ hours or until the lamb is tender and falling away
from the bone.

2. Remove from heat and stir in parsley. Use tongs to
remove the bones. Taste and season with salt and
pepper. Ladle soup into bowls and serve with crusty
bread.

Lentil soup with frankfurters

SERVES
6

INGREDIENTS

1 cup (9 fl oz) green lentils, rinsed

2 rashers bacon, diced

1 leek, washed and finely diced

1 large carrot, diced

1 stalk celery, diced

1 tablespoon vegetable oil

1 onion, finely chopped

1 tablespoon plain (all-purpose) flour

1 tablespoon vinegar

4 Frankfurters, thinly sliced

1 tablespoon tomato sauce

1 teaspoon salt

¼ teaspoon freshly ground black pepper

METHOD

1. Place lentils in a large saucepan, add water and bring slowly to the boil.

2. Add bacon, leek, carrot and celery, partly cover and allow to simmer for 30 minutes.

3. In a small frying pan, heat the oil, add onion and sauté until golden. Stir in flour, lower the heat and stir until flour turns a light golden colour. Sir in a few spoonfuls of soup stock and mix until smooth and free of lumps. Stir in vinegar then add contents of pan to soup. Cover and simmer for 30 minutes. If soup is thickening more than desired, add a little water.

4. Add sliced Frankfurters, tomato sauce, salt and pepper. Simmer for 5 minutes, taste and adjust seasoning to taste. Serve with rye bread.

Pork and vegetable soup

SERVES
4

INGREDIENTS

400 g (14 oz) boneless pork, cut into 15 mm (½ in) cubes

2 tablespoons plain (all-purpose) flour

1 tablespoon vegetable oil

1 medium onion, chopped

2 stalks celery, diced

3 cups chicken stock

½ teaspoon dried marjoram

2 medium potatoes, peeled and diced

125 g (4 oz) mushrooms, chopped

½ medium green capsicum (bell pepper), chopped

1 small carrot chopped

2 tablespoons diced pimiento

¼ cup flat-leaf parsley, chopped

METHOD

1. Place pork and flour in a plastic bag and shake until coated.
2. Heat oil in a large saucepan. Add the pork and brown lightly. Add chopped carrot and onion and sauté.
3. Sauté 2–3 minutes longer. Add celery, stock and marjoram. Bring to the boil. Cover and simmer for 15 minutes.
4. Add potatoes and mushrooms. Bring to the boil again. Cover and simmer for 10 minutes. Stir in green capsicum and pimiento. Simmer for 5 minutes more.
5. Sprinkle with parsley. Ladle into bowls.

Lamb shank and barley soup

SERVES
8

INGREDIENTS

4 lamb shanks, fat removed

6 cups (50 fl oz) beef stock

1 teaspoon salt

½ cup barley, washed

2 medium onions, finely diced

2 medium carrots, medium diced

2 stalks celery, thinly sliced

1 small turnip, medium diced

freshly ground black pepper

¼ cup parsley, chopped

METHOD

1. Bring the lamb shanks, stock and salt to the boil. Add barley and bring back to the boil.

2. Skim off any froth from the surface, cover and gently simmer over low heat for 2–3 hours. Add vegetables and simmer for a further 30 minutes.

3. Remove the shank bones, chop the meat and return to the soup. Season with salt and pepper, garnish with parsley and serve.

Turkish wedding soup

SERVES
8

INGREDIENTS

1 kg (2 lb 4 oz) lamb shanks, bones broken

¼ cup seasoned flour

1 tablespoon oil

60 g (2 oz) butter

1 onion, grated

salt and freshly ground black pepper

3 egg yolks

¼ cup lemon juice

1½ teaspoons paprika

pinch of cayenne pepper

METHOD

1. Coat the shanks in seasoned flour. Heat oil and half the butter, add shanks and cook until brown. Add 6 cups (50 fl oz) water, bring to the boil, and skim off the froth.

2. Reduce heat, add the onion, salt and pepper and simmer covered for 2 hours or until the lamb is tender. Allow to cool and refrigerate overnight.

3. Skim off the fat, strain into a saucepan and discard the onion. Remove meat from the shanks. Chop meat and return to the stock.

4. Add egg yolks and lemon juice and cook, without boiling. Melt the remaining butter and stir in paprika and cayenne pepper. Garnish with the paprika mixture and serve.

Middle Eastern spinach and meatball soup

SERVES
4

INGREDIENTS

50 g (9 oz) minced lamb

1 large brown onion, finely minced

2 cloves garlic, minced

salt and freshly ground black pepper

2 tablespoons olive oil

2 large leeks, sliced

1 tablespoon ground turmeric

1 tablespoon ground cinnamon

120 g (4 oz) yellow split peas

6 cups (50 fl oz) vegetable stock

500 g (17½ oz) spinach, chopped

400 g (14 oz) potatoes, peeled and cubed

4 tablespoons rice flour

juice of 2 lemons

3 tablespoons natural yoghurt

4 French shallots, sliced

10 mint leaves, finely sliced

METHOD

1. Mix together the lamb, minced onion, garlic and lots of salt and pepper, then shape the meat mixture into walnut-size balls and refrigerate for 30 minutes.

2. Heat the olive oil and add the leeks to the saucepan, sautéing until they are golden. Add the turmeric and cinnamon and continue stirring and cooking until the mixture is fragrant, about 2 minutes. Add the split peas and stock and bring to the boil. Simmer for 30 minutes.

3. Add the meatballs to the soup and simmer for 10 minutes. Add the spinach and potato cubes and continue simmering for 10 minutes.

4. Mix the rice flour with a little water and the lemon juice and whisk until smooth, then drizzle this mixture into the soup. Season and simmer for 10 more minutes.

5. Finally, fold through the yoghurt, being careful not to let the soup boil. Heat a little extra oil then fry the shallot slices until crisp and deep golden brown. Garnish the soup with the fried shallots and the finely sliced mint leaves.

Meatballs in egg and lemon soup

SERVES
4

INGREDIENTS

500 g (17½ oz) beef mince

1 medium onion, finely
chopped

¼ cup parsley, chopped

¼ cup (2¼ oz) medium-grain
rice

2 eggs

salt and freshly ground
black pepper

⅓ cup (2¾ oz) cornstarch
(cornflour)

4 cups (35 fl oz) beef stock

50 g (1¾ oz) butter

⅓ cup lemon juice

METHOD

1. Combine the mince, onion, parsley, rice and 1 egg in a bowl, and mix well with your hands. Season well with salt and pepper. Using one tablespoon of mixture for each meatball, shape mixture into balls. Roll in cornstarch, shaking off any excess.

2. Bring the stock and the butter to the boil, then reduce the heat and place the meatballs in the stock. Cover and simmer for 45 minutes. Allow to cool slightly.

3. Whisk the remaining egg and lemon juice together in a bowl, then add ½ cup (4 fl oz) of warm stock. Pour this mixture back into the saucepan and heat very gently. Season with salt and pepper before serving.

Harira

SERVES
8

INGREDIENTS

500 g (1 lb 2 oz) lamb, cut into small cubes

1 teaspoon turmeric

1 teaspoon freshly ground black pepper

1 teaspoon ground cinnamon

¼ teaspoon ground ginger

30 g (1 oz) butter

2 stalks celery and leaves, chopped

2 onions, chopped

¼ cup fresh parsley

¼ cup fresh coriander (cilantro), chopped

800 g (1 lb 10 oz) canned chopped tomatoes

1 teaspoon salt

¾ cup (6½ oz) lentils

1 cup canned chickpeas, drained and rinsed

¼ cup vermicelli

2 eggs

juice of ½ lemon

METHOD

1. Put the lamb, spices, butter, celery, onion, parsley and coriander in a large saucepan and stir over a low heat for 5 minutes. Drain the tomatoes and reserve the juice, add the tomato flesh to the saucepan and continue cooking for 10–15 minutes. Salt lightly.

2. Add the juice from the tomatoes, 7 cups water and the lentils. Bring to the boil, then reduce heat, partially cover, and simmer for 2 hours.

3. When ready to serve, add the chickpeas and vermicelli and cook for 5 minutes. Beat the eggs with the lemon juice then, with the soup at a steady simmer, stir the lemony eggs into the stock with a long wooden spoon. Continue stirring slowly to create long egg strands and to thicken the soup. Season to taste, ladle into bowls and dust with cinnamon. Serve the extra lemon in a side bowl if desired.

Russian cabbage soup

SERVES
6

INGREDIENTS

30 g (1 oz) butter

250 g (9 oz) beef, diced

125 g (4 oz) bacon pieces

300 g (10½ oz) cabbage,
finely shredded

2 large tomatoes, peeled
and diced

2 onions, diced

1 potato peeled and
chopped

1 bay leaf

salt and freshly ground black
pepper

4 cups (35 fl oz) beef stock

⅓ cup (3 fl oz) sour cream

40 g (1½ oz) Parmesan
cheese, grated

METHOD

1. Melt butter in a large saucepan and sauté beef and
   bacon over a medium heat until browned.

2. Add half the cabbage and all the remaining ingredients
   except sour cream and Parmesan. Cover, bring to the
   boil, and simmer for 1½ hours. Add remaining cabbage
   and cook for 10–15 minutes or until tender. Stir in cream,
   sprinkle with Parmesan cheese and serve.

Hearty beef and barley soup

SERVES 8

INGREDIENTS

¹⁄3 cup wholewheat flour

1 teaspoon salt

500 g (17½ oz) lean stewing beef

2 tablespoons olive oil

1 medium onion, chopped

4 large cloves garlic, minced

½ medium carrot, grated

1 stalk celery, chopped

1 large tomato, diced

1 cup (9 oz) barley

5 cups (44 fl oz) chicken stock

¼ cup basil, chopped

1 bay leaf

salt and freshly ground black pepper

METHOD

1. In a plastic bag, combine flour, salt and meat. Shake vigorously.

2. In a large saucepan, pour in the oil and quickly brown the meat over medium heat. Add onions and garlic and cook until soft, about 3–4 minutes. Add the carrot, celery and tomato and continue cooking for about 5 minutes.

3. Add barley, stock and basil and bring to the boil. Wrap the bay leaf in cheesecloth and add to the pot. Lower heat and allow to simmer until the barley is soft, about 20–25 minutes.

4. Season to taste with the salt and pepper. Remove bay leaf before serving.

Vegetable beef soup

SERVES
8

INGREDIENTS

2 kg (4 lb 6 oz) beef shanks

2 tablespoons olive oil

1 teaspoon salt

1 small onion, chopped

450 g (15 oz) canned diced
  tomatoes

6 sprigs parsley

5 carrots, sliced

100 g (3½ oz) green beans,
  cut diagonally

1 medium potato, diced

1 stalk celery, chopped

¼ cup (2¼ oz) barley

METHOD

1. In a heavy-based frying pan, brown the meat in the olive oil. Pour off excess fat and oil.

2. Cover with 8 cups (70 fl oz) cold water and bring to the boil. Add salt and onion, simmer for 2 hours.

3. Add vegetables and barley. Simmer for about 1 hour longer. Remove meat from bone, add back to soup and serve.

Hungarian goulash soup

SERVES
8

INGREDIENTS

3 tablespoons olive oil

2 medium white onions, sliced

2 tablespoons Hungarian (mild) paprika

2 cloves garlic, minced

2 teaspoons caraway seeds

8 sprigs fresh marjoram, leaves removed and stalks discarded

500 g (17½ oz) diced beef

400 g (14 oz) canned diced tomatoes

2 tablespoons tomato paste

6 cups (50 fl oz) beef stock

2 teaspoons brown sugar

1 teaspoon salt

1 teaspoon pepper

400 g (14 oz) potatoes, diced

200 g (7 oz) carrots, diced

1 tablespoon cornstarch (cornflour), mixed with 2 tablespoons cold water

METHOD

1. Heat the olive oil in a saucepan and sauté the onion until golden brown, about 5 minutes. Add the paprika, garlic, caraway seeds and marjoram and cook for 1–2 minutes until the mixture is fragrant.

2. Add the beef, diced tomatoes and tomato paste, and cook until the meat is well coated and is a rich brown colour, about 5 minutes. Add the stock, sugar, salt and pepper and bring to the boil. Simmer for 1 hour. Add the potatoes, carrots and continue cooking for a further 30 minutes.

3. Check seasonings and adjust if necessary. Stir the cornstarch mixture into the soup, mixing well. Allow the soup to thicken for a couple of minutes, then serve in individual bowls.

Jewish goulash soup

SERVES
6-8

INGREDIENTS

2 tablespoons olive oil

1 medium white onion, sliced

1 tablespoon Hungarian paprika

2 cloves garlic, minced

2 teaspoons caraway seeds

zest of ½ lemon

4 sprigs fresh oregano, leaves removed and chopped

500 g (17½ oz) diced beef

2 tablespoons tomato paste

5 cups (44 fl oz) beef stock

2 teaspoons brown sugar

2 bay leaves

1 teaspoon salt

1 teaspoon pepper

500 g (17½ oz) potatoes, peeled and diced

2 pickled cucumbers, finely diced

¼ cup (2¼ oz) sour cream

METHOD

1. Heat the olive oil and sauté the onion until golden brown, about 5 minutes. Add the paprika, garlic, caraway seeds, lemon zest and oregano and cook for a minute or two. Add the beef and tomato paste, and cook until the meat is well coated and is a rich brown colour, about 5 minutes.

2. Add the stock, sugar, bay leaves, salt and pepper and bring to the boil. Simmer for 1 hour.

3. Add the potatoes and continue cooking for a further 30 minutes. Check seasonings and adjust if necessary. Remove bay leaves. Serve in individual bowls, garnished with sour cream and finely diced cucumbers.

Balinese egg noodle soup

SERVES
6-8

SOUP

6 French shallots

2 cloves garlic

4 cm (1½ in) piece fresh ginger

2 carrots, julienned

1 sweet potato, julienned

150 g (5 oz) Chinese cabbage, shredded

8 cups (70 fl oz) chicken or vegetable stock

8 spring onions (scallions), green parts only, julienned

100 g (3½ oz) dried egg noodles

1 tablespoon sweet soy sauce

2 onions, sliced and fried until crisp

1 red capsicum (bell pepper), finely shredded

MEATBALLS

2 tablespoons olive oil

250 g (9 oz) minced beef

2 teaspoons ground coriander (cilantro)

1 egg white

1 tablespoon cornstarch (cornflour)

salt and freshly ground black pepper

METHOD

1. Peel and finely chop the shallots, garlic and ginger. Heat the oil and sauté until these flavourings are softened. Remove one-third of this mixture and reserve for the meatballs.

2. To the remaining mixture, add the carrots and sweet potato and sauté for 5 minutes. Add the shredded cabbage and cook until wilted, about 4 minutes. Add the chicken or vegetable stock and the scallion greens and bring to the boil.
Simmer for 10 minutes.

3. Meanwhile, make the meatballs. To the reserved shallot mixture, add the minced meat, cilantro, egg white, cornstarch, salt and pepper to taste. Mix well and form into small balls.

4. To the simmering soup, add the meatballs and allow to boil gently for a further 5 minutes. Add the noodles, pushing them down into the soup, and simmer for a further 2 minutes or until the noodles are just tender.

5. Season with the sweet soy sauce and serve garnished with fried onions and red bell pepper.

Oxtail soup

SERVES
8

INGREDIENTS

1 oxtail

1 tablespoon seasoned flour

2 tablespoons oil

6 cups (50 fl oz) beef stock

1 carrot, sliced

1 small turnip, sliced

1 onion, roughly chopped

2 stalks celery, chopped

2–3 bay leaves

salt

pinch of cayenne pepper

juice of 1 lemon

1 teaspoon Worcestershire
sauce

3 tablespoons sherry or
Madeira

METHOD

1. Coat oxtail in seasoned flour. Heat oil over a medium heat, add oxtail and cook until brown. Add stock and simmer for 2 hours. Skim off the froth.

2. Place vegetables and bay leaves in the stock and cook for a further 15–20 minutes.

3. Remove meat from bones, return the meat to soup and reheat. Season with salt and cayenne pepper. Stir in lemon juice and Worcestershire sauce. Just before serving, add sherry.

COLD SOUPS

How about a delightful iced soup to cool the palate on a very hot and stressful day? Or just sit around the pool, relax with a good book, and you will find that an iced soup is just the ticket to get the taste buds going. Try our Gazpacho with just a hint of chilli or a creamy Vichyssoise to soothe the nerves.

Chilled asparagus soup

SERVES
6

INGREDIENTS

300 g (10½ oz) very green
asparagus spears

4 cups (35 fl oz) chicken
stock

40 g (1½ oz) butter

40 g (1½ oz) plain (all-
purpose) flour

2 cups(17 fl oz) heated milk

½ cup (4 fl oz) thickened
cream

15 g (½ oz) Parmesan cheese

METHOD

1. Remove the woody end from the spears. Place the asparagus in a saucepan and cover with chicken stock. Bring to the boil and cook for 10 minutes.

2. Remove the asparagus and chop off and reserve some of the tips for garnish. Purée the asparagus and then strain. Reserve the strained pulp. Reduce the chicken stock to a quarter by boiling at high heat.

3. In a separate saucepan, melt the butter and add the flour. Combine and remove from the heat after 2 minutes. Add the milk and stir constantly to ensure there are no lumps.

4. Add the reduced chicken stock and asparagus pulp. Stir well and return to the heat. Stir frequently for 10 minutes.

5. Add the cream and the cheese. Season with salt and pepper if necessary. Chill thoroughly and if the colour is a little insipid, add some green colouring. Garnish with reserved asparagus tips.

Chilled dill soup

SERVES
4

INGREDIENTS

2 cups (17 fl oz) vegetable stock

1 large onion, chopped

4 zucchini (courgette), chopped

1 large potato, chopped

½ teaspoon ground cumin

1 cup (9 fl oz) sour cream

2 tablespoons chopped fresh dill

sprigs fresh dill

METHOD

1. Place stock, onion, courgette, potato and cumin in a large saucepan and bring to the boil. Reduce heat and simmer for
20 minutes or until potatoes are tender. Remove saucepan from heat and set aside to cool slightly.

2. Place soup mixture in a food processor or blender and process until smooth. Transfer soup to a large bowl, stir in sour cream and dill, then cover and chill for 3 hours before serving. Ladle soup into chilled bowls and garnish with dill sprigs.

Hot & Cold Soups

GAZPACHO

**SERVES
6–8**

INGREDIENTS

2 slices of stale bread

2 kg (4 lb 6 oz) tomatoes, roughly chopped

1 cucumber, peeled and chopped

1 green capsicum (bell pepper), deseeded and chopped

1 small onion, chopped

2 cloves garlic, chopped

5 tablespoons olive oil

1–2 tablespoons wine vinegar

1 teaspoon cumin seeds or ground cumin

METHOD

1. Soak bread in a little water, and squeeze it out before using (the bread helps to thicken the soup and give it a nice consistency).

2. Blend all vegetables and garlic in a blender or food processor, and push through a sieve into a bowl. Use the blender again to beat bread, oil and vinegar together. Add some of the tomatoes, the cumin seeds and salt to taste. Add a little water and mix into the bowl with the soup. Add a few ice cubes and leave to become cold. You can add more water if necessary.

Traditionally this soup was made by crushing the ingredients with a mortar and pestle and then adding cold water. Gazpacho traditionally should be served in wooden bowls and eaten with a wooden spoon. You can make large quantities of gazpacho as it keeps well.

Chilled apricot soup

SERVES
6

INGREDIENTS

800 g (1 lb 12 oz) canned
   apricot halves, puréed

juice of 1 lemon

juice of 1 orange

2 cups (17 fl oz) white wine

pinch of nutmeg

¼ cup mint leaves

METHOD

1. Combine all ingredients except mint and mix well.

2. Place into a glass bowl and refrigerate for 2 hours. Serve chilled, garnished with mint leaves.

Iced Curried Fruit Soup

SERVES
6

INGREDIENTS

2 cooking apples, cored and roughly chopped, plus

1 peeled and coarsely grated

1 banana, chopped

125 g (4½ oz) papaya, peeled, deseeded and chopped

4 green onions, finely chopped

2 cups (17 fl oz) tomato juice

1 cup chicken stock

½ teaspoon curry powder

salt and freshly ground black pepper

1 cup (9 fl oz) thickened cream

3 tablespoons shredded coconut

cooked strips of pappadum

METHOD

1. Place the chopped apples, banana, papaya and green onions in a food processor or blender and process until smooth. Blend in the tomato juice, stock and curry powder. Pour into a large jug or bowl, adjust the seasonings and leave to chill for several hours.

2. Place the cream in a bowl, beat until soft peaks form, and then fold in the coconut and grated apple. Leave to chill. Serve the soup with a spoonful of cream mixture and pappadum strips.

To cook pappadums, heat 2 cups of oil in a high-sided frying pan or medium saucepan until hot. Add 1 pappadum – it will quickly puff up and become golden. Remove it from the oil immediately and drain it on absorbent paper. Repeat with the remaining pappadums.

Summer Herb Soup

SERVES 6

INGREDIENTS

2 tablespoons olive oil

1 large Spanish onion, chopped

1kg zucchini (courgette), chopped

1 cup fresh coriander (cilantro)leaves

1 cup fresh parsley leaves

1 cup fresh basil leaves

4 cups (35 fl oz) chicken stock

1 cup extra herbs (e.g. dill, coriander, basil, parsley etc.)

juice and zest of 1 lemon

sour cream or yoghurt, to serve

freshly ground black pepper, to serve

METHOD

1. In a large saucepan, heat the oil and add the chopped onion. Cook until the onion softens then add the chopped zucchini and herbs, stirring well to incorporate, then continue to cook for 5 minutes.

2. Add the chicken stock and simmer for 20 minutes until the zucchini is tender. Add the cup of extra fresh herbs and stir briefly.

3. Add the lemon juice and zest then purée the soup with a food processor or hand-held 'wand' until smooth and serve at room temperature or chilled, garnished with a swirl of sour cream or yoghurt and black pepper and extra chopped herbs.

Peach cooler

SERVES
8

INGREDIENTS

5 very ripe peaches, peeled, stoned and roughly chopped

juice of 1 lemon

1 teaspoon caster sugar

750 ml (24 fl oz) dry white wine

1 small bay leaf

1 clove

1 small piece of cinnamon stick

pinch of salt

½ cup whipped cream

sprigs of fresh mint

METHOD

1. Purée the peaches with the lemon juice and sugar. Add the wine, bay leaf, clove, cinnamon stick and salt and bring to the boil over a low heat.

2. Chill thoroughly and strain before serving. Garnish with a spoonful of cream, sprinkle with fresh mint and serve.

Pumpkin vichyssoise

SERVES 6

INGREDIENTS

500 g (17½ oz) peeled, deseeded butternut pumpkin

250 g (9 oz) leek, chopped and washed

8 cups (70 fl oz) chicken stock

1 teaspoon salt

¼ teaspoon cayenne pepper

½ teaspoon paprika

½ cup thickened cream

¼ small bunch chives, chopped

METHOD

1. Place pumpkin, leek, and stock in a boiling pot and place over a high heat. Boil until the pumpkin has broken down.

2. Remove from the heat and add the salt, cayenne pepper and paprika. Blend or process to a very fine consistency, check seasoning.

3. Chill for 2–3 hours before service.

4. To serve, add cream and garnish with chopped chives.

Chilled yoghurt soup

SERVES
4–6

INGREDIENTS

1 large telegraph cucumber

1 cup (9 fl oz) thickened cream

200 ml (7 fl oz) natural yoghurt

2 tablespoons white wine vinegar

1 tablespoon balsamic vinegar

¼ cup fresh mint, chopped

1 clove garlic, crushed

salt and freshly ground black pepper

METHOD

1. Peel and grate the cucumber.

2. Combine the cream, yoghurt and vinegars, and whisk lightly, until smooth. Stir in the cucumber, mint, garlic and seasoning. Cover and chill for three hours.

3. Stir and taste for seasoning before serving chilled. Garnish with a slice of cucumber, a sprig of mint and cracked pepper.

Iced tomato soup

SERVES
8

INGREDIENTS

3 slices bread, crusts removed

1 kg (2 lb 4 oz) tomatoes, peeled, deseeded and chopped

1 cucumber, peeled, deseeded and chopped

½ onion, chopped

2 cloves garlic, crushed

½ green capsicum (bell pepper), deseeded and chopped

1 teaspoon salt

1 teaspoon ground cumin

2 tablespoons olive oil

2 tablespoons wine vinegar

GARNISH

1 red or green capsicum (bell pepper), diced

1 small cucumber, diced

1 onion, finely chopped

2 hard-boiled eggs

chopped croutons

METHOD

1. Place all ingredients in a large bowl and allow to stand for 30 minutes to soften bread and blend flavours.

2. Purée one-third of the mixture at a time in an electric blender or food processor. Pour back into a bowl and thin down to desired consistency with 2–3 (17-26 fl oz) cups iced water.

3. Cover and chill well. Adjust seasoning to taste. Serve in chilled bowls or in a large bowl over ice.

4. Place garnish ingredients in separate bowls and allow each diner to add garnish to their own soup.

Dill and Cucumber Soup

SERVES 6

INGREDIENTS

500 ml (17 fl oz) milk

2 leeks, cleaned and chopped

2 cloves garlic, peeled and sliced

2 fresh bay leaves (or dried)

1 teaspoon black peppercorns

4 cloves garlic

6 continental cucumbers

2 tablespoons butter or olive oil

1 fennel bulb, finely sliced

2 tablespoons fresh dill

salt and black pepper

2 tablespoons plain flour

600 ml (21 fl oz) rich chicken or vegetable stock

150 ml (5 fl oz) sour cream

100 ml (3½ oz) thick yoghurt

2 tablespoons fresh dill, snipped

METHOD

1. Place the milk in a medium saucepan and add the chopped leeks, sliced garlic, bay leaves, peppercorns and cloves and bring the milk to the boil. When the milk is about to boil, remove the pan from the heat and allow the milk to infuse for 1 hour. Strain and reserve the milk and discard the solids.

2. Meanwhile, peel five of the cucumbers and cut them in half, lengthways. Remove the seeds with a teaspoon then slice the cucumber halves. Blanch the cucumber pieces in boiling water for one minute then immediately drain.

3. Heat the butter or olive oil in a large saucepan and add the sliced fennel and dill and cook for two minutes. Add salt and pepper to taste and the blanched cucumbers and sauté them for about 20 minutes or until the vegetables are soft and golden. Add the flour and toss well until the flour has been absorbed. Add the stock and reserved infused milk and gently bring the soup to the boil. Simmer for 30 minutes or until the soup is fragrant (don't worry if the soup has a curdled appearance at this stage). Purée until smooth then cool thoroughly.

4. Adjust seasoning then fold through the sour cream and yoghurt. Finely dice the remaining unpeeled cucumber and garnish the soup with the cucumber pieces and snipped dill.

Chilled Green Tomato Soup

SERVES
6

INGREDIENTS

1½ kg (3 lb 5 oz) green tomatoes

3 cups (26 fl oz) rich vegetable stock

½ cup fresh dill

½ cup fresh coriander (cilantro)

½ cup (4 fl oz) thick Greek yoghurt

salt and pepper to taste

100 g (3½ oz) Bulgarian fetta cheese

fresh dill, snipped, to serve

METHOD

1. Place the chopped tomatoes and stock in a saucepan and simmer for 10 minutes.

2. Add the herbs and stir well. Purée the soup with the yoghurt until smooth and balance the flavour with salt and pepper to taste then chill until ready to serve.

3. To serve, ladle the soup into individual bowls and top with crumbled fetta and extra dill.

Moroccan Spiced Cold Tomato Soup

SERVES
4

INGREDIENTS

1 small onion, chopped

2 tablespoons olive oil

1 teaspoon paprika

¼ teaspoon ground ginger

¼ teaspoon ground cumin

¼ teaspoon ground cinnamon

400 g (14 oz) canned chopped tomatoes

1¾ cups (15 fl oz) chicken stock

2 teaspoons honey

¼ cup fresh parsley, chopped

¼ cup fresh coriander (cilantro), chopped

½ teaspoon lemon juice

salt and freshly ground black pepper

1 lemon, cut into slices

METHOD

1. Cook onion in oil with spices in a 3-litre (105½ fl oz) saucepan over moderate heat, stirring occasionally, until onion is softened and begins to brown, about 4–5 minutes.

2. Add tomatoes to onion mixture with the stock, honey and half the parsley and coriander, then bring to the boil.

3. Transfer soup to a metal bowl set in a larger bowl of ice-cold water. Cool soup until cold, stirring occasionally.

4. Stir in lemon juice and salt and pepper to taste, then stir in remaining parsley and coriander. Serve garnished with lemon slices.

Rock Melon Soup

SERVES
4

INGREDIENTS

1 large rock melon, halved
  and seeds removed

60 g (2¼ oz) butter

2 teaspoons sugar

grated zest of 1 lemon

pinch of salt

3 cups (26 fl oz) milk

sprigs of mint

METHOD

1. Using a melon baller, scoop out 12 balls of melon and reserve. Coarsely chop the remaining flesh.

2. Heat the butter over a low heat, add the coarsely chopped melon, sugar, lemon zest and salt and simmer for 4 minutes. Add milk and bring to the boil.

3. Purée mixture and chill well. Garnish with reserved melon balls and mint sprigs and serve.

Vichyssoise

SERVES
4

INGREDIENTS

60 g (2 oz) butter

2 leeks, washed and thinly
sliced

1 medium onion, thinly sliced

500 g (17½ oz) potatoes,
peeled and sliced

3 cups (26 fl oz) chicken
stock

salt and freshly ground
black pepper

¾ cup thickened cream

¼ small bunch chives,
chopped

METHOD

1. Melt butter in a saucepan, add leeks and onion and
sauté until tender without browning. Add potatoes,
stock and seasonings and simmer until soft. Purée.

2. Chill for 2–3 hours. Adjust seasonings, stir in the cream
and serve in chilled bowls garnished with chopped
chives.

Summer chill

SERVES
4

INGREDIENTS

2 cucumbers

2 green apples, peeled and cored

2 tablespoon lemon juice

1 cup (9 fl oz) dry white wine

1 teaspoon sugar

METHOD

1. Peel the cucumbers, reserving the peel. Purée cucumber flesh, apple and sufficient cucumber peel to give a pale green colour. Add remaining ingredients and mix well. Chill with ice block, garnish with extra sliced apple and cucumber and serve immediately.

Pineapple,Capsicum and Dill Soup

SERVES
6-8

INGREDIENTS

1 medium pineapple, cored, peeled and chopped

2 small Continental cucumbers, peeled, deseeded and chopped

1 cup (9 fl oz) pineapple juice

1 cup (9 fl oz) apple juice

juice of 1 lemon

1 red capsicum (bell pepper), finely diced

1 yellow capsicum (bell pepper), finely diced

2 small red birds-eye chillies

1 medium red onion, finely sliced

¼ cup fresh dill, chopped

¼ cup flat-leaf parsley, chopped, plus 6 whole sprigs

salt and freshly ground black pepper

1 tablespoon olive oil

1 teaspoon Tabasco sauce

METHOD

1. Place the peeled and chopped pineapple,chopped cucumbers, pineapple juice, applejuice, lemon juice, half the red and yellow capsicum, the chillies, onion, dill and parsley ina blender or food processor and process untilalmost smooth.

2. Transfer the mixture to a bowl and seasonto taste with salt and pepper then chill untilready to serve.

3. Heat a little oil then fry the parsley sprigs until bright green and brittle. Drain on absorbent paper.

4. Ladle the soup into bowls and sprinkle with remaining yellow and red capsicum and deep-fried parsley sprigs. Drip the Tabasco sauce into the soup, around the garnish, then serve.

Chilled Red Capsicum & Fennel Soup

SERVES
8

INGREDIENTS

2 tablespoons olive oil

2 leeks, white part only, chopped

1 Spanish onion, chopped

2 cloves garlic, chopped

2 shallots, chopped

5 large carrots, chopped

2 fennel bulbs, halved, cored and chopped

4 sprigs fresh thyme

2–3 red capsicums (bell peppers)

1 cup (9 fl oz) white wine

4½ cups (39½ fl oz) light chicken stock or vegetable stock

salt and freshly ground pepper

3 tablespoons mild yoghurt

MINTED CORN SALSA

2 ears of corn

½ small Spanish onion, finely diced

1 Roma tomato, seeded

10 fresh mint leaves, finely sliced

2 sprigs fresh coriander (cilantro), chopped

⅓ cup chopped fresh parsley

juice of 1 lime

salt and freshly ground pepper

METHOD

1. Heat olive oil in a saucepan and add the leeks, onion, garlic and shallots and sweat for 5 mins until soft. Add the carrots, fennel and thyme sprigs and cook over medium heat for 30 mins until all vegetables are soft.

2. Slice the whole capsicums (discard the seed core) and grill skin side up for 5 mins. Transfer the capsicums into a plastic bag and allow to steam. When cool open bag and slip skins off.

3. Add capsicum pieces, white wine and stock to the softened vegetables and rise heat to high and continue to cook uncovered for 20 mins until combined. Remove the soup from the heat and purée with food blender. Season to taste with salt and pepper and allow to cool in fridge for one hour.

4. Make the salsa by cutting all the corn off the ears and microwaving on high for 2 mins. Mix the onion, tomato and corn in a bowl and add mint leaves, coriander, parsley, lime juice. Add salt and pepper as desired. Mix well.

Hot & Cold Soups

Beetroot and Orange Soup

SERVES
6

INGREDIENTS

3 large beetroots, peeled
and grated

1 small onion, finely chopped

8 cups (70 fl oz) chicken
stock

juice of 3 large oranges

2 teaspoons salt

pinch of cayenne pepper

1 orange, sliced

¼ cup parsley, chopped

METHOD

1. Boil the beetroot and onion in the chicken stock for
   15 minutes.

2. Remove from the heat and add the orange juice, salt
   and cayenne pepper.

3. Return to the heat and cook for 5 minutes. Serve hot or
   chilled with slices of orange floating in the centre and
   sprinkled with chopped parsley.

Watercress and potato soup

SERVES
4

INGREDIENTS

1 medium bunch watercress, coarsely chopped

1 kg (2 lb 4 oz) potatoes, peeled and roughly chopped

4 cups (35 fl oz) milk

1¼ cups (11 fl oz) vegetable stock

salt and freshly ground black pepper

chopped fennel leaves

croutons and sour cream, for garnish

METHOD

1. Simmer the potatoes in the milk and stock. Add the watercress when the potatoes are nearly cooked, then cook for a further 10 minutes.

2. Purée the ingredients in a blender or food processor. Season with salt and pepper, and chill completely. Serve with the chopped fennel or dill leaves. Garnish with croutons and sour cream.

INDEX

First published in 2017 by New Holland Publishers
This edition published in 2022 by New Holland Publishers
Auckland • Sydney

newhollandpublishers.com

Level 1, 178 Fox Valley Road, Wahroonga 2076, Australia
5/39 Woodside Ave, Northcote, Auckland 0627, New Zealand

ISBN 9781760794743

Group Managing Director: Fiona Schultz
Project Editor: Jessica Nelson
Designer: Yolanda La Gorcé
Production Director: Arlene Gippert

Printed in China

10 9 8 7 6 5 4 3 2 1

Keep up with New Holland Publishers:
 NewHollandPublishers
 @newhollandpublishers

US $16.99